Lovingkindness

LOVINGKINDNESS

The Revolutionary Art of Happiness

25TH ANNIVERSARY EDITION

Sharon Salzberg

FOREWORD BY
Jon Kabat-Zinn

SHAMBHALA · *Boulder* · 2020

Shambhala Publications, Inc.
4720 Walnut Street
Boulder, Colorado 80301
www.shambhala.com

©1995 by Sharon Salzberg
Foreword ©1995 by Jon Kabat-Zinn
Afterword ©2020 by Sharon Salzberg
Page 173 constitutes an extension of this copyright page. All rights reserved. No part of this book may be reproduced in any form or by any means, electronic or mechanical, including photocopying, recording, or by any information storage and retrieval system, without permission in writing from the publisher.

9 8 7 6 5 4 3 2 1

Printed in the United States of America

♾ This edition is printed on acid-free paper that meets the American National Standards Institute z39.48 Standard.
♻ This book is printed on 30% postconsumer recycled paper. For more information please visit us at www.shambhala.com.

Shambhala Publications is distributed worldwide by Penguin Random House, Inc., and its subsidiaries.

The Library of Congress catalogues the previous edition of this book as follows:
Salzberg, Sharon.
Lovingkindness: the revolutionary art of happiness/ Sharon Salzberg.—1st ed.
p. cm.
ISBN 978-1-57062-037-9 (hardcover)
ISBN 978-1-57062-176-5 (paperback)
ISBN 978-1-57062-903-7 (Shambhala Classics)
ISBN 978-1-61180-624-3 (Shambhala Pocket Library)
ISBN 978-1-61180-820-9 (25th anniversary edition)
1. Meditation—Buddhism. 2. Compassion (Buddhism)
1. Title.
BQ5612.S25 1995   94-30379
294.3´443—dc20 CIP

This is what should be done
By those who are skilled in goodness,
And who know the path of peace:
Let them be able and upright,
Straightforward and gentle in speech.
Humble and not conceited,
Contented and easily satisfied.
Unburdened with duties and frugal in their ways.
Peaceful and calm, and wise and skillful,
Not proud and demanding in nature.
Let them not do the slightest thing
That the wise would later reprove.
Wishing: in gladness and in safety,
May all beings be at ease.
Whatever living beings there may be;
Whether they are weak or strong, omitting none,
The great or the mighty, medium, short or small,
The seen and the unseen,
Those living near and far away,
Those born and to-be-born—
May all beings be at ease!
Let none deceive another,
Or despise any being in any state.
Let none through anger or ill-will
Wish harm upon another.
Even as a mother protects with her life
Her child, her only child,
So with a boundless heart
Should one cherish all living beings;
Radiating kindness over the entire world:
Spreading upward to the skies,
And downward to the depths;
Outward and unbounded,
Freed from hatred and ill-will.

Whether standing or walking, seated or lying down,
Free from drowsiness,
One should sustain this recollection.
This is said to be the sublime abiding.
By not holding to fixed views,
The pure-hearted one, having clarity of vision,
Being freed from all sense desires,
Is not born again into this world.

>—The Buddha's words on lovingkindness
>*(Metta Sutta)*

Contents

Foreword by Jon Kabat-Zinn   ix
Acknowledgments   xi
Introduction   1

1. The Revolutionary Art of Happiness   7
2. Relearning Loveliness   17
   EXERCISE *Remembering the Good within You*   25
   EXERCISE *Phrases of Lovingkindness*   26
3. Facets of Lovingkindness   29
   EXERCISE *The Benefits of Lovingkindness*   39
   EXERCISE *The Benefactor*   39
4. Hindrances to Lovingkindness   41
   EXERCISE *Reflection on Happiness*   49
   EXERCISE *The Meaning of Friends*   50
   EXERCISE *The Beloved Friend*   50
   EXERCISE *The Neutral Person*   51
5. Working with Anger and Aversion   53
   EXERCISE *Forgiveness*   63
   EXERCISE *Seeing Goodness*   65
   EXERCISE *The Difficult Person*   66
   EXERCISE *Difficult Aspects of Oneself*   69

6. Breaking Open the Loving Heart 71
   EXERCISE *Lovingkindness for All Beings* 83
   EXERCISE *Lovingkindness toward Groups* 84
   EXERCISE *Walking Meditation* 85
   EXERCISE *The Ten Directions* 85

7. Developing the Compassionate Heart 87
   EXERCISE *Meditation on Compassion* 98
   EXERCISE *Compassion for Those Who Cause Pain* 99

8. Liberating the Mind through Sympathetic Joy 101
   EXERCISE *Meditation on Sympathetic Joy* 113
   EXERCISE *Sharing Merit* 114

9. The Gift of Equanimity 115
   EXERCISE *Equanimity* 128

10. The Power of Generosity 131
    EXERCISE *Giving* 142

11. Living Our Love 145
    EXERCISE *The Practice of Morality* 160

Afterword to the 25th Anniversary Edition 165
For More Information 171
Credits 173
About the Author 175

Foreword

MANY OF SHARON SALZBERG'S readers will know that over the main portal of the Insight Meditation Society in Barre, Massachusetts, where she teaches, is inscribed in large letters the word *metta*, Pali for "lovingkindness." Some may have wondered, as I have on occasion, why that particular word is up there rather than, say, *mindfulness* or *insight* or *equanimity* or *wisdom* or *compassion*. For me, in the end, all these qualities, which we cultivate in meditation practice on long retreats at places such as IMS and in our daily lives wherever we find ourselves, distill down to this simple quality of heart and whether and how we allow it to express itself in the minute daily conduct of our lives, both toward ourselves and toward others.

The Dalai Lama has said: "My religion is kindness." If we all adopted such a stance and embodied it in thought and action, inner and outer peace would be immediate, for in reality they are never not present, only obscured, waiting to be discovered. This is the work and the power of lovingkindness, the embrace that allows no separation between self, others, and events—the affirmation and honoring of a core goodness in others and in oneself. The practice of lovingkindness is, in fact, the ground of mindfulness practice, requiring the same nonjudging, nongrasping, nonrejecting orientation toward the present moment, an orientation that invites and makes room for calmness, clarity of mind and heart, and understanding.

In this book, Sharon shows us how we might systematically cultivate lovingkindness in our lives. Given the pain and turmoil that we often experience, the endemic misperceptions of the human mind regarding who and what we are, and how we relate to the stress and pain of our lives, practicing lovingkindness is an arduous discipline—no less so than attending to one's breathing or observing the stream of one's thought. But it is an extremely effective path, a fundamental path in the opening of mind and heart. In it are to be found the seeds of profound happiness, inner well-being, and healing for ourselves and for all the beings, human and otherwise, all miraculous, with whom we share this fragile living planet. May this book help further that process far and wide.

—Jon Kabat-Zinn
July 1994

Acknowledgments

Those teachers, friends, and students who in the course of my life have helped me learn about lovingkindness are too numerous to mention. Some who have specifically aided me with this book are as follows.

Steve Smith and Alan Clements, who first inspired me to go to Burma. Rand Engel, who suggested I write a book on lovingkindness. Joseph Goldstein, who has gone with me on every turn of this path and most recently taught me how to handle troublesome chapters.

Barbara Gates, who edited with enormous grace and skill, and taught me some essential elements of writing. Ann Barker, Sarah Doering, Catherine Ingram, Kate Wheeler, Judith Stanton, and Dorothy Austin, who offered me unflagging support as well as editorial suggestions and creative consults. The staff and teachers of IMS, who devote themselves to these teachings.

Eric Kolvig, who began the project with me, whose outstanding editing skills made it all possible, and who made critical contributions to several chapters. David Berman, who taught me six of the seven things I can do on a computer, who heroically flew back in the middle of winter to help, and who helped unstintingly right through to the end.

The writers' club: Tara Bennett-Goleman, Susan Harris, Dan Goleman, Ram Dass, Kedar Harris, and Joseph Goldstein, who contributed continual inspiration and some helpful peer pressure. Susan Harris for the gift of a computer and a revolutionary friendship. Tara Bennett-Goleman and Kate Wheeler, who generously spent so many hours contemplating titles. Anasuya Weil, who did so much transcribing, and who never stopped asking me about the book.

Kedar Harris, who was absolutely fearless in saying what he thought, and whose comments on my early versions were all too true. Jack Kornfield, who has been my advocate. Shoshana Alexander, who put aside her own work to so beautifully facilitate the flow of mine through her unique editorial abilities. Surya Das, who lugged my computer through LaGuardia, and who introduced me to people who recast my knowledge of love and compassion.

Lovingkindness

Introduction

THROUGHOUT OUR LIVES we long to love ourselves more deeply and to feel connected with others. Instead, we often contract, fear intimacy, and suffer a bewildering sense of separation. We crave love, and yet we are lonely. Our delusion of being separate from one another, of being apart from all that is around us, gives rise to all of this pain. What is the way out of this?

Spiritual practice, by uprooting our personal mythologies of isolation, uncovers the radiant, joyful heart within each of us and manifests this radiance to the world. We find, beneath the wounding concepts of separation, a connection both to ourselves and to all beings. We find a source of great happiness that is beyond concepts and beyond convention. Freeing ourselves from the illusion of separation allows us to live in a natural freedom rather than be driven by preconceptions about our own boundaries and limitations.

The Buddha described the spiritual path that leads to this freedom as "the liberation of the heart which is love," and he taught a systematic, integrated path that moves the heart out of isolating contraction into true connection. That path is still with us as a living tradition of meditation practices that cultivate love, compassion, sympathetic joy, and equanimity. These four qualities are among the most beautiful and powerful states of consciousness we can experience. Together they are called in Pali, the language spoken by the Buddha, the *brahma-vihara*s. *Brahma* means "heavenly." *Vihara* means "abode" or "home." By practicing these meditations, we establish love (Pali, *metta*), compassion (*karuna*), sympathetic joy (*mudita*), and equanimity (*upekkha*) as our home.

I first encountered the practice of the brahma-viharas when I was introduced to Buddhism in 1971 in India. I had joined many other people in what turned out to be a significant migration of Westerners seeking the spiritual teachings of the East. I was very young, but my longing for a deeper understanding of life and of the suffering I had already endured drew me there.

One thing we did encounter was more suffering as we faced the extremes of climate and tropical illnesses of India. Several years later, after a number of us had founded the Insight Meditation Society in Barre, Massachusetts, a friend with whom I had spent several years in India was talking to one of the physicians working at the local clinic in Barre. She was describing the terrible heat in the summers of New Delhi, when the temperature can exceed 110 degrees. One summer, when she was trying to renew her visa, she was forced to go from government office to government office in that intense heat. My friend was explaining to the doctor that she had been especially weak that summer because she was just recovering from being afflicted with hepatitis, amoebic dysentery, and worms. I can remember the doctor looking at her, absolutely appalled, and saying, "You had all those diseases and you were trying to renew your visa! What were you doing, holding out for leprosy?"

On the face of it our sojourn in India was indeed a story of disease, discomfort, and a heroic effort (or foolish determination) to carry on. But despite those physical sufferings my friend was relating, I know that her internal experience was one of sheer magic. Our time in India, completely outside of our customary social pretenses or mannered responses, allowed each of us an entirely new look at ourselves. Through meditation practice, many of us came into initial contact with our own capacity for goodness and felt the elation of discovering a new connection with all beings. I cannot imagine anything that I would be willing to trade for that discovery—no money, no power over others, no trophies or accolades.

That year, sitting under the Bodhi Tree in Bodh Gaya, where the Buddha attained enlightenment, I voiced my aspiration to realize the gift of love that the Buddha himself had realized and embodied. The brahma-viharas—love, compassion, sympathetic joy, and equanimity—are that very gift, and the opportunity to practice them is the legacy of the Buddha. By following this path we learn to develop skillful mental states and let go of unskillful ones.

The integrity we develop on a spiritual path comes from being able to distinguish for ourselves the habits and influences in the mind which are skillful and lead to love and awareness, from those which are unskillful and reinforce our false sense of separation. The Buddha once said:

> Abandon what is unskillful. One *can* abandon the unskillful. If it were not possible, I would not ask you to do it. If this abandoning of the unskillful would bring harm and suffering, I would not ask you to abandon it. But as it brings benefit and happiness, therefore I say, abandon what is unskillful.
>
> Cultivate the good. One *can* cultivate the good. If it were not possible, I would not ask you to do it. If this cultivation were to bring harm and suffering, I would not ask you to do it. But as this cultivation brings benefit and happiness, I say, cultivate the good.

Abandoning unskillful states that cause suffering is not something we do out of fear of or contempt for those states, or out of contempt for ourselves for having those states arise in the mind. Abandoning the unskillful isn't accomplished by angrily shoving or pushing away our habits of separation. Rather it comes as we learn to truly love ourselves and all beings, so that love provides the light by which we bear witness to those burdens, watching them simply fall away.

Rather than obsessively following states of mind such as anger, fear, or grasping, states that will bring harm to ourselves and others, we can let go as though dropping a burden. We are indeed burdened by carrying around habitual unskillful reactions. As wisdom reveals to us that we don't need these reactions, we can abandon them.

Cultivating the good means recovering the incandescent power of love that is present as a potential in all of us. An awakened life demands a fundamental re-visioning of the limited views we hold of our own potential. To say that we cultivate the good means that we align ourselves with an expansive vision of what is possible for us, and we use the tools of spiritual practice to sustain our real, moment-to-moment experience of that vision.

This vision is always available to us; it doesn't matter how long we may have been stuck in a sense of our limitations. If we go into a darkened room and turn on the light, it doesn't matter if the room has been dark for a day, or a week, or ten thousand years—we turn on the light and it is illumined. Once we contact our capacity for love and happiness—the good—the light has been turned on. Practicing the brahma-viharas is a way of turning on the light and then tending it. It is a process of deep spiritual transformation.

This transformation comes from actually walking the path: putting the values and theories into practice, bringing them to life. We make the effort to abandon the unskillful and cultivate the good with the conviction that in fact we can be successful. "If it were not possible, I would not ask you to do it." Remembering this statement of the Buddha, we walk the path knowing that each of us is capable of actualizing our singular potential for love and truth.

The path begins with cultivating appreciation of our oneness with others through generosity, nonharming, right speech, and right action. Then, on the foundation of these qualities, we purify our minds through the concentration practices of meditation. As we do, we come to experience wisdom through recognizing the truth, and become deeply aware of the suffering caused by separation and of the happiness of knowing our connection with all beings. The culmination of this recognition is called by the Buddha "the sure heart's release." Coming to an understanding of the true nature of the heart and of happiness is the fulfillment of a spiritual path. The practice of the brahma-viharas is both a means to this understanding and a natural expression of it.

My own intensive practice of the four brahma-viharas began in Burma in 1985. Under the guidance of Sayadaw U Pandita, a Theravada meditation master, my days were completely devoted to nurturing and cultivating love, compassion, sympathetic joy, and equanimity. What extraordinary days! That protected period of retreat so clarified and strengthened the brahma-viharas that when the retreat was over, I found that they did not erode but had truly become my home. At times, of course, I lose touch with these qualities, but my homing instinct for happiness now brings me back to them.

In this book I offer the meditative techniques I first encountered in India and later systematically learned in Burma. All of my teachers, since the time I first started to practice Buddhism, have each in their own way shown me the blessing of lovingkindness and the sense of great possibility it provides. This book comes out of tremendous appreciation for each one of them. The meditative techniques presented here are offered out of the immense gratitude I feel for having had the opportunity to learn these practices, and out of the wish that others may benefit from them.

1
The Revolutionary Art of Happiness

Only connect.
—*E. M. Forster*

WE CAN TRAVEL a long way and do many different things, but our deepest happiness is not born from accumulating new experiences. It is born from letting go of what is unnecessary, and knowing ourselves to be always at home. True happiness may not be at all far away, but it requires a radical change of view as to where to find it.

A meditator at one of our first retreats found this out in a very pointed way. Before we established the center of the Insight Meditation Society, we had to rent sites for long meditation retreats. For our first one, we rented a monastery with a beautiful chapel. In order to turn the chapel into a meditation hall where we could sit on the floor, we had to remove all the pews and store them in a large back room. Owing to a shortage of sleeping accommodations, one of the meditators slept in a corner of that back room for the duration of the retreat.

During the course of the retreat this meditator began to experience a lot of aches and pains. Feeling quite annoyed and disturbed by them, he spent a long time searching the monastery for the perfect chair, one that would allow him to sit without pain. Unable to find it, he decided that his only recourse was to sneak into the monastery workshop at night to build himself a chair. He meticulously planned how he would do this without being discovered. Then, confident that he would soon have the solution to his problems, he went to the workshop to look over the tools and materials available. Back in the room where he was staying, he sat down on one of the pews stored there and set about designing the absolutely perfect meditation chair, guaranteed to end suffering.

As he was sitting there working, he realized that he was feeling happier and happier. At first he thought the happiness came because he was creating the unheralded, revolutionary, perfect design. Then suddenly he realized that, in fact, he was so happy because he was remarkably comfortable sitting on one of the pews. He looked around and saw that there were about three hundred of those pews right in his own room. What he was looking for had been right in front of him all along. Instead of taking that tortuous mental journey, he could have just sat down.

Sometimes we take quite a journey—physically or mentally or emotionally—when the very love and happiness we want so much can be found by just sitting down. We spend our lives searching for something we think we don't have, something that will make us happy. But the key to our deepest happiness lies in changing our vision of where to seek it. As the great Japanese poet and Zen master Hakuin said, "Not knowing how near the Truth is, people seek it far away. What a pity! They are like one who, in the midst of water, cries out in thirst so imploringly."

Ordinary happiness comes from the experience of pleasure—the satisfaction, for a little while, of getting what we want. Such happiness is like the temporary appeasement of an unhappy, insatiable child. We reach out for the consolation of a momentary distraction, and then we are upset when it changes. I have a friend who is four years old. When he gets frustrated, or does not get what he wants, the hallways of his house echo with his cries: "Nobody loves me anymore!" We as adults often feel the same: when we do not get what we want—or when we get what we want, only to have it change—it seems as though all the love in the universe has been withdrawn from us. Happiness becomes an either/or situation. Just like those of the four-year-old, our interpretations and judgments obstruct clear seeing.

Life is just as it is, despite our protests. For all of us there is a constant succession of pleasurable and painful experiences. Once

I was hiking with friends in Northern California. We had decided beforehand to follow a certain trail for the first three days, and then to retrace our steps for the next three. On the third day of this arduous hike, we found ourselves on a long, steady downhill slope. After several hours of this, one of my friends, suddenly realizing what all this walking downhill implied for the next day when we would be retracing our steps, turned to me and said glumly, "In a dualistic universe, downhill can mean only one thing."

The unrelenting flux of life's changing conditions is inevitable, yet we labor to hold on to pleasure, and we labor equally hard to avoid pain. So many images from our world tell us that it is wrong to suffer; advertising, social mores, and cultural assumptions suggest that feeling pain or sadness is blameworthy, shameful, humiliating. Underlying these messages is an expectation that somehow we should be able to control pain or loss. When we experience mental or physical pain, we often feel a sense of isolation, a disconnection from humanity and life. Our shame sets us apart in our suffering at the very times when we need most to connect.

Conventional transitory happiness carries a subtle undercurrent not only of loneliness but also of fear. When things are going well, when we are experiencing pleasure and are getting what we want, we feel obliged to defend our happiness because it seems so fragile, unstable. As though our happiness needed constant protection, we deny the very possibility of suffering; we cut ourselves off from facing it in ourselves and in others because we fear that it will undermine or destroy our good fortune. Thus, in order to hold on to our pleasure, we refuse to recognize the humanity of a homeless person on the street. We decide that the suffering of others is not relevant to our own lives. We cut ourselves off from facing the world's suffering because we fear it will undermine or destroy our own happiness. In that highly defended state, we withdraw into so terrible an aloneness that we cannot experience true joy. How strange our conditioning is: to feel so alone in our pain, and to feel so vulnerable and isolated in our happiness.

For some people, a single powerful experience may propel them out of this isolation. Ashoka was an emperor in northern India about two hundred and fifty years after the time of the Buddha. In the early years of his reign, this powerful emperor was bloodthirsty and greedy for the expansion of his empire. He was also a very unhappy man. One day, after a particularly terrible battle that he had launched in order to acquire more territory, he walked on the battlefield amid the appalling spectacle of corpses of men and animals strewn everywhere, already rotting in the sun and being devoured by carrion-eating birds. Ashoka was aghast at the carnage he had caused.

Just then a Buddhist monk came walking across the battlefield. The monk did not say a word, but his being was radiant with peace and happiness. Seeing that monk, Ashoka thought, "Why is it that I, having everything in the world, feel so miserable? Whereas this monk has nothing in the world apart from the robes he wears and the bowl he carries, yet he looks so serene and happy in this terrible place."

Ashoka made a momentous decision on that battlefield. He pursued the monk and asked him, "Are you happy? If so, how did this come to be?" In response, the monk who had nothing introduced the emperor who had everything to the Buddha's teachings. As a consequence of this chance encounter, Ashoka devoted himself to the practice and study of Buddhism and changed the entire nature of his reign. He stopped waging imperialistic wars. He no longer allowed people to go hungry. He transformed himself from a tyrant into one of history's most respected rulers, acclaimed for thousands of years after as just and benevolent.

Ashoka's own son and daughter carried Buddhism from India to Sri Lanka. The teachings took root there and from India and Sri Lanka spread to Burma and Thailand and throughout the world. Our access to these teachings today, so many centuries and cultural transitions later, is a direct result of Ashoka's transformation. The radiance of that one Buddhist monk is still affecting the world today. One person's serenity changed the course of history, and delivered to us the Buddhist path to happiness.

The basis of the Buddha's psychological teaching is that our efforts to control what is inherently uncontrollable cannot yield the security, safety, and happiness we seek. By engaging in a delusive quest for happiness, we only bring suffering upon ourselves. In our frantic search for something to quench our thirst, we overlook the water all around us and drive ourselves into exile from our own lives.

We may look for that which is stable, unchanging, and safe, but awareness teaches us that such a search cannot succeed. Everything in life changes. The path to true happiness is one of integrating and fully accepting all aspects of our experience. This integration is represented in the Taoist symbol of yin/yang, a circle which is half dark and half light. In the midst of the dark area is a spot of light, and in the midst of the light area is a spot of darkness. Even in the depths of darkness, the light is implicit. Even in the heart of light, the dark is understood, acknowledged, and absorbed. If things are not going well for us in life and we are suffering, we are not defeated by the pain or closed off to the light. If things are going well and we are happy, we are not defensively trying to deny the possibility of suffering. This unity, this integration, comes from deeply accepting darkness and light, and therefore being able to be in both simultaneously.

The English writer E. M. Forster began one of his novels with a two-word epigraph: "Only connect." These two words perfectly express the shift we must make, from one worldview to another, if we are to find reliable happiness. We must move from trying to control the uncontrollable cycles of pleasure and pain, and instead learn how to connect, to open, to love no matter what is happening.

The difference between misery and happiness depends on what we do with our attention. Do we, in the midst of water, look for something elsewhere to drink? Transformation comes from looking deeply within, to a state that exists before fear and isolation arise, the state in which we are inviolably whole just as we are. We connect to ourselves, to our own true experience, and discover there that to be alive means to be whole.

Consider how the sky is unharmed by the clouds that pass through it, whether they are light and fluffy-looking or dark and formidable. A mountain is not moved by the winds blowing over it, whether gentle or fierce. The ocean is not destroyed by the waves moving on its surface, whether high or low. In just that way, no matter what we experience, some aspect of ourselves remains unharmed. This is the innate happiness of awareness.

There is a word in Buddhist psychology, *tathata*, that can be translated as "thusness" or "suchness." It describes a state in which the totality of our being is present; our awareness is not fragmented or divided. In the state of suchness, some part of ourselves is not sitting elsewhere waiting for something better or different to happen. We are not relating to our experience with either desire or aversion, but rather we accept what comes into our lives and let go of what leaves our lives. We are completely present and not beguiled by the token happiness promised by conventional assumptions. In experiencing the freedom of suchness, we discover who we actually are.

A friend of mine once traveled to Sikkim, hoping to see His Holiness the Sixteenth Karmapa, a great Tibetan lama. The trip to Sikkim was quite arduous, demanding the crossing of great mountain passes and the fording of rivers. Having made this effort, my friend was delighted to be actually granted an audience with His Holiness. He was amazed to find that the Karmapa, an eminent spiritual leader known the world over, treated him as though his visit were one of the most important things that had ever happened to the Karmapa in his life. This treatment did not manifest through grandiose gestures or ceremony, but rather through the simplicity and completeness of the Karmapa's presence, which offered my friend an experience of being completely loved. When I heard this story, I thought about how many conversations I have had during which my attention was halfhearted. I might be thinking about the next thing I had to do or the next person I had to talk to. How unfair that lack of attention now seems! The simple act of being completely present to another person is truly an act of love—no drama is required.

Just being with someone who, like the Karmapa, manifests this kind of genuine presence is a call for us to awaken to our true nature. Such a person is complete in him- or herself, needing nothing from us, offering no ground for our projections to land upon. Where could projection and manipulation exist in such a relationship? We look into the mirror of his or her eyes and recognize ourselves, and all that is possible for us.

Sometimes I meet an extraordinary, loving teacher. In the first moment of seeing him or her I realize, "Oh, that's who I really am!" I feel a deep recognition of the innate and inviolate power of love within me as well. And I also see that many concepts about myself, my fears and desires, are superimposed over that power, concealing it. These concepts dissolve in the presence of such a person; I awaken for a moment and can say, "Oh, right, that's who I really am. That's what's right and possible for all beings." These encounters disprove my seeming limitations, and I walk free for a while from a prison that I once fabricated for myself.

Completeness and unity constitute our most fundamental nature as living beings. That is true for all of us. No matter how wonderful or terrible our lives have been, no matter how many traumas and scars we may carry from the past, no matter what we have gone through or what we are suffering now, our intrinsic wholeness is always present, and we can recognize it.

This recognition breaks the spell of conventional thought. Surrendering our fixations, simply being happy, is like suddenly breaking free from confinement. It is as if we were in a small, cramped room on top of a mountain, and all at once the walls have come tumbling down, revealing a panoramic vista. How breathtaking!

This is the opening we have yearned for and looked for in so many places: in relationship, at work, and in society. Because this opening can happen without dependence on another person or any external situation for its fulfillment, there is the bliss of security in it, of safety and inviolability. The mind becomes radiant, luminous in unification, open, with nothing held back and nothing to add, not fragmented, no more divisions.

Great fullness of being, which we experience as happiness, can also be described as love. To be undivided and unfragmented, to be completely present, is to love. To pay attention is to love.

The great Indian teacher Nisargadatta Maharaj once said, "Wisdom tells me I am nothing. Love tells me I am everything. Between the two my life flows." "I am nothing" does not mean that there is a bleak wasteland within. It does mean that with awareness we open to a clear, unimpeded space, without center or periphery—

THE REVOLUTIONARY ART OF HAPPINESS   13

nothing separate. If we are nothing, there is nothing at all to serve as a barrier to our boundless expression of love. Being nothing in this way, we are also, inevitably, everything. "Everything" does not mean self-aggrandizement, but a decisive recognition of interconnection; we are not separate. Both the clear, open space of "nothing" and the interconnectedness of "everything" awaken us to our true nature.

This is the truth we contact when we meditate, a sense of unity beyond suffering. It is always present; we merely need to be able to access it. Knowing this truth through direct experience, we enjoy a profound change in our sense of ourselves, of the world, and of life itself. We can also call unity health. The very word *health* means "whole." Our deepest health, beyond even life and death, lies in our inherent completeness, integration, and connectedness.

Much of the time, rather than feeling whole, we may feel fragmented and disconnected, and therefore unhealthy on one level or another. During the course of the day we experience ourselves in many different roles, maybe as a wife, an employee, a friend, a daughter. When we are alone we have one image of ourselves; when we are with other people we have another image. With people we know, we act one way; with those we do not know, we act differently. We feel fragmented and estranged from ourselves, so our gestures of friendship to others are often born out of loneliness and fear. Looking for trust and closeness, we end up finding only the appearance of relationship.

Contrast our predicament with this haiku of Issa:

In the cherry blossom's shade
there's no such thing
as a stranger.

In touch with our wholeness, with a heart filled with love, there is no such thing as a stranger, not in ourselves or in others. In the expanse of true happiness, there is nowhere for fragmentation to take root.

An enlightened being such as the Buddha symbolizes that quality of health, freedom, love—the highest aspirations of humankind.

Whether the Buddha was alone or with people, whether he was teaching and serving or living in solitude, he was effortlessly aware of wholeness. His happiness was not bound to any particular situation, subject to change. The Thai meditation master Ajahn Chah describes this happiness which we can attain through meditation practice: "Your mind will become still in any surroundings, like a clear forest pool. All kinds of wonderful, rare animals will come to drink at the pool, and you will clearly see the nature of all things. You will see many strange and wonderful things come and go, but you will be still. This is the happiness of the Buddha." The unbounded happiness of the Buddha was founded on the clear seeing and compassion running through his life in all circumstances. This is "suchness."

This happiness transforms us within and revolutionizes our perspective on the world without. In fact, the concept of within and without itself disappears.

Resting fully in the present is the source of this happiness. We open to our own experience, and inevitably that opens us to others. To be truly happy in this world is a revolutionary act because true happiness depends upon a revolution in ourselves. It is a radical change of view that liberates us so that we know who we are most deeply and can acknowledge our enormous ability to love. We are liberated by the truth that every single one of us can take the time and pay attention; we can be the Karmapa; we can be that monk walking across the battlefield. That is our birthright. Our own happiness can change history, and it does.

2

Relearning Loveliness

The bud
stands for all things,
even for those things that don't flower,
for everything flowers, from within, of self-blessing;
though sometimes it is necessary
to reteach a thing its loveliness,
to put a hand on the brow
of the flower,
and retell it in words and in touch,
it is lovely
until it flowers again from within, of self-blessing
. . . .

—*Galway Kinnell*

"To reteach a thing its loveliness" is the nature of metta. Through lovingkindness, everyone and everything can flower again from within. When we recover knowledge of our own loveliness and that of others, self-blessing happens naturally and beautifully.

Metta, which can be translated from Pali as "love" or "lovingkindness," is the first of the brahma-viharas, the "heavenly abodes." The others—compassion, sympathetic joy, and equanimity—grow out of metta, which supports and extends these states.

In our culture, when we talk about love, we usually mean either passion or sentimentality. It is crucial to distinguish metta from both of these states. Passion is enmeshed with feelings of desire, of wanting or of owning and possessing. Passion gets entangled with needing things to be a certain way, with having our expectations met. The expectation of exchange that underlies most passion is both conditional and ultimately defeating: "I will love you as long as you behave in the following fifteen ways, or as long as you love me in return at least as much as I love you." It is not a coincidence that the word *passion* derives from the Latin word for "suffering." Wanting and expectation inevitably entail suffering.

By contrast, the spirit of metta is unconditional: open and unobstructed. Like water poured from one vessel to another, metta flows freely, taking the shape of each situation without changing its essence. A friend may disappoint us; she may not meet our expectations, but we do not stop being a friend to her. We may in fact disappoint ourselves, may not meet our own expectations, but we do not cease to be a friend to ourselves.

Sentimentality, the other mental state that masquerades as love, is really an ally of delusion. It is a facsimile of caring that limits itself only to experiences of pleasure. Like looking through the lens of a camera that has been smeared with a little Vaseline, sentimentality puts things into what is called "soft focus." We cannot see the rough edges, the trouble spots, or the defects. Everything appears just too nice. Sentimentality finds pain unbearable and so rejects it.

Our vision becomes very narrow when we need things to be a certain way and cannot accept things the way they actually are. Denial functions almost as a kind of narcotic, so that vital parts of our lives end up missing.

It is fear of pain that provokes and sustains this splitting off of parts of ourselves. To avoid feeling pain, we shut out crucial portions of awareness, even though this closing off, this internal separation, is deadening.

Sometimes as individuals, or as members of a group, we may sacrifice the truth in order to secure our identity, or preserve a sense of belonging. Anything that threatens this gives rise to fear and anxiety, so we deny, we cut off our feelings. The end result of this pattern is dehumanization. We become split from our own lives and feel great distance from other living beings as well. As we lose touch with our inner life, we become dependent on the shifting winds of external change for a sense of who we are, what we care about, and what we value. The fear of pain that we tried to escape becomes, in fact, our constant companion.

The Buddha first taught the metta meditation as an antidote to fear, as a way of surmounting terrible fear when it arises. The legend is that he sent a group of monks off to meditate in a forest that was inhabited by tree spirits. These spirits resented the presence of the monks and tried to drive them away by appearing as ghoulish visions, with awful smells and terrible, shrieking noises. The tradition says that the monks became terrified and ran back to the Buddha, begging him to send them to a different forest for their practice. Instead, the Buddha replied, "I am going to send you back to the same forest, but I will provide you with the only protection you will need." This was the first teaching of metta meditation. The Buddha encouraged the monks not only to recite the metta phrases but to actually practice them. As these stories all seem to end so happily, so did this one—it is said that the monks went back and practiced metta, so that the tree spirits became quite moved by the beauty of the loving energy filling the forest, and resolved to care for and serve the monks in all ways.

The inner meaning of the story is that a mind filled with fear can still be penetrated by the quality of lovingkindness. Moreover, a mind that is saturated by lovingkindness cannot be overcome by fear; even if fear should arise, it will not overpower such a mind.

When we practice metta, we open continuously to the truth of our actual experience, changing our relationship to life. Metta—the sense of love that is not bound to desire, that does not have to pretend that things are other than the way they are—overcomes the illusion of separateness, of not being part of a whole. Thereby metta overcomes all of the states that accompany this fundamental error of separateness—fear, alienation, loneliness, and despair—all of the feelings of fragmentation. In place of these, the genuine realization of connectedness brings unification, confidence, and safety.

In Buddhism there is one word for mind and heart: *chitta*. Chitta refers not just to thoughts and emotions in the narrow sense of arising from the brain, but also to the whole range of consciousness, vast and unimpeded. As we open to the experience of chitta, we come to an understanding of who we are, with an ability to care for ourselves. Through the force of love, the presumed boundaries between ourselves and others crumble into ash as we touch them.

What unites us all as human beings is an urge for happiness, which at heart is a yearning for union, for overcoming our feelings of separateness. We want to feel our identity with something larger than our small selves. We long to be one with our own lives and with each other.

If we look at the root of even the most terrible addictions, even the most appalling violence in this world, somewhere we will find this urge to unite, to be happy. In some form it is there, even in the most distorted and odious disguises. We can touch that. We can draw near and open up. We can connect, to the difficult forces within ourselves, and to the different experiences in our lives. We can break through the concepts that keep us apart. This is the true nature of love and the source of healing for ourselves and our world. This is the ground of freedom.

Metta is the ability to embrace all parts of ourselves, as well as all parts of the world. Practicing metta illuminates our inner integrity because it relieves us of the need to deny different aspects of ourselves. We can open to everything with the healing force of love. When we feel love, our mind is expansive and open enough to include the entirety of life in full awareness, both its pleasures and its pains. We feel neither betrayed by pain nor overcome by it, and thus we can contact that which is undamaged within us regardless of the situation. Metta sees truly that our integrity is inviolate, no matter what our life situation may be. We do not need to fear anything. We are whole: our deepest happiness is intrinsic to the nature of our minds, and it is not damaged through uncertainty and change.

In cultivating love, we remember one of the most powerful truths the Buddha taught—that the mind is naturally radiant and pure. It is because of visiting defilements that we suffer.

The word *defilement* is a common translation of the Pali word *kilesa*, which more literally translated means "torment of the mind." We know directly from our own experience that when certain states arise strongly within us, they have a tormenting quality—states like anger, fear, guilt, and greed. When they knock at the door and we invite them in, we lose touch with the fundamentally pure nature of our mind, and then we suffer.

By not identifying with these forces, we learn that these defilements or torments are only visitors. These forces are adventitious, not inherent. They do not reflect who we really are. The defilements or the kilesas inevitably arise because of how we have been conditioned. But this is no reason to judge ourselves harshly. Our challenge is to see them for what they are and to remember our true nature.

We can understand the inherent radiance and purity of our minds by understanding metta. Like the mind, metta is not distorted by what it encounters. Anger generated within ourselves or within others can be met with love; the love is not ruined by the anger. Metta is its own support, and thus it is free of inherently unstable conditions. The loving mind can observe joy and peace in one moment, and then grief in the next moment, and it will not be shattered by the change. A mind filled with love can be likened to the sky with a variety of clouds moving through it—some light and fluffy, others ominous and threatening. No matter what the situation, the sky is not affected by the clouds. It is free.

The Buddha taught that the forces in the mind that bring suffering are able to temporarily hold down the positive forces such as love or wisdom, but they can never destroy them. The negative forces can never uproot the positive, whereas the positive forces can actually uproot the negative forces. Love can uproot fear or anger or guilt, because it is a greater power.

Love can go anywhere. Nothing can obstruct it. *I Am That*, a book of dialogues with Nisargadatta Maharaj, includes an exchange between Nisargadatta and a man who complained a great deal about his mother. The man felt that she had not been a very good mother and was not a good person. At one point, Nisargadatta advised him to love his mother. The man replied, "She wouldn't let me." Nisargadatta responded, "She couldn't stop you."

No external condition can prevent love; no one and no thing can stop it. The awakening of love is not bound up in things being a certain way. Metta, like the true nature of the mind, is not dependent; it is not conditioned. When we practice meditation and perceive this quality of mind, we also contact the essence of metta. This produces a tremendous change in perspective. At first it is as if we were sitting on the shore and watching waves dance on the surface of the ocean. Later in meditation it is as if we are underwater, in the calm, still depths, watching the waves above us moving and playing. Still later we perceive that, in fact, we *are* the water, not apart or separate, and that waving is happening. This is also how metta embraces all.

The Pali word *metta* has two root meanings. One is the word for "gentle." Metta is likened to a gentle rain that falls upon the earth. This rain does not select and choose—"I'll rain here, and I'll avoid that place over there." Rather, it simply falls without discrimination.

The other root meaning for *metta* is "friend." To understand the power or the force of metta is to understand true friendship. The Buddha actually described at some length what he meant by being a good friend in the world. He talked about a good friend as someone who is constant in our times of happiness and also in our times of adversity or unhappiness. A friend will not forsake us when we are in trouble nor rejoice in our misfortune. The Buddha described a true friend as being a helper, someone who will protect us when we are unable to take care of ourselves, who will be a refuge to us when we are afraid.

Once, when someone described to the Dalai Lama how much fear they were experiencing in their meditation practice, he said, "When you're afraid, just put your head in the lap of the Buddha." The lap of the Buddha epitomizes the safety of a true friendship. The culmination of metta is to become such a friend to oneself and all of life.

The practice of metta, uncovering the force of love that can uproot fear, anger, and guilt, begins with befriending ourselves. The foundation of metta practice is to know how to be our own friend. According to the Buddha, "You can search throughout the entire universe for someone who is more deserving of your love and affection than you are yourself, and that person is not to be found anywhere. You yourself, as much as anybody in the entire universe, deserve your love and affection." How few of us embrace ourselves in this way! With metta practice we uncover the possibility of truly respecting ourselves. We discover, as Walt Whitman put it, "I am larger and better than I thought. I did not think I held so much goodness."

Directly seeing the natural radiance of our minds reteaches us our own loveliness. To allude to a phrase in the Zen tradition, this is our original face before we were born—before we were born into identification with a separate, limited self. Recognizing our own power to love points us directly to recognizing this primordial radiance.

Confidence in our innate potential to be loving human beings empowers the cultivation of metta. Our potential to love is very real and is somehow not destroyed, no matter what we experience: all of the mistakes that we might make, all of the times that we are caught in reaction, all of the times we have caused pain, all of the times we have suffered. Throughout everything, our potential to love remains intact and pure. Through practicing metta in meditation and in daily life, we cultivate this potential. Love joins with our intention, as partners in healing ourselves and our world.

In some ways our greatest ally in this practice of love is our wish to be happy. This wish functions as a homing instinct for freedom when we can unite it with understanding what actually brings us happiness. But sometimes we may feel that we do not really deserve happiness; we may feel almost ashamed of wanting it. Yet this wish is one of the finest things about us, opening the door to transcending our limited lives.

In certain philosophical systems in India during the Buddha's time, it was believed that if the body was tortured enough, abused enough, the spirit would soar free and be liberated. Nowadays most of us are not inclined to torture our bodies to free our spirits. However, we do seem to have our own variation of that theme by believing that if we abuse our minds enough with self-hatred and self-condemnation, somehow that abuse will be a path that liberates us.

For a true spiritual transformation to flourish, we must see beyond this tendency to mental self-flagellation. Spirituality based on self-hatred can never sustain itself. Generosity coming from self-hatred becomes martyrdom. Morality born of self-hatred becomes rigid repression. Love for others without the foundation of love for ourselves becomes a loss of boundaries, codependency, and a painful and fruitless search for intimacy. But when we contact, through meditation, our true nature, we can allow others to also find theirs.

We so often in our lives serve as mirrors for one another. We look to others to find out if we ourselves are lovable; we look to others to find out if we are capable of feeling love; we look to others for a reflection of our innate radiance. What a tremendous gift, to enable someone's return to the awareness of their own loveliness! When we see the goodness in others, we are enabling them to "flower from within, of self-blessing."

Seeing the goodness in someone does not imply ignoring their difficult qualities or unskillful actions. Rather, we can fully acknowledge these difficulties, while at the same time we choose to focus on the positive. If we focus on the negative, we will naturally feel anger, resentment, or disappointment. If we focus on the positive, we will forge a connection to the person. Then as we look at their negative traits or actions, we do it as their friend. If two friends are looking at such difficult things, they do so standing side by side.

This mirroring quality, whereby we "reteach a thing its loveliness," is one of the greatest attributes of metta. The power of metta enables us to look at people and affirm the rightness of their wish to be happy; it affirms our oneness with them. The power of love reflects both to ourselves and others the manifold possibilities available in each moment.

I once heard a young man talk about his life as a child in Cambodia. All of the children in his village spent years imprisoned in a barbed-wire encampment. Four times a day people were brought to the outskirts of that encampment to be killed. The children were all lined up and forced to watch. According to the rule, if one of them started to cry, then he or she would also be killed. This boy said that each time people were brought to be killed, he was absolutely terrified that among them would be a friend, neighbor, or relative. He knew that if that happened, he would start to cry, and then he would be killed himself. He lived with this terror for years. He said that in that circumstance, the only way he could survive was to completely cut off all feeling, to dehumanize himself altogether.

After many years the political situation changed in Cambodia, and this boy was adopted by an American family and brought to the United States. At that point in his life, he knew that now he would be able to survive only if he learned to love again, to break down the walls that he had been forced to create. The young man related that he learned to love again by looking into the eyes of his foster father and seeing there so much love for him. In the mirror of his foster father's love, the boy realized that he was indeed lovable, and that therefore he was also capable of extending love.

Looking at people and communicating that they can be loved, and that they can love in return, is giving them a tremendous gift. It is also a gift to ourselves. We see that we are one with the fabric of life. This is the power of metta: to teach ourselves and our world this inherent loveliness.

Metta binds all beings together. Buddhist psychology identifies it as the cohesive factor in consciousness. When a person experiences anger, the heart is dry. It becomes moist when that person feels love. When we put together two substances in nature that are dry, they cannot cohere; there is no way for them to join. When we add wetness, these two substances can bond; they can come together. In just that same way, the force of metta, lovingkindness, allows us to cohere, to come together within ourselves and with all beings. The beauty of this truth moved the Buddha to say that sustaining a loving heart, even for the duration of the snap of a finger, makes one a truly spiritual being.

EXERCISE
Remembering the Good within You

Sit comfortably, in a relaxed way, and close your eyes. As much as possible, let go of analysis and expectation. For ten to fifteen minutes, call to mind something you have done or said that you feel was a kind or good action—a time you were generous, or caring, or contributed to someone's well-being. If something comes to mind, allow the happiness that may come with the remembrance. If nothing comes to mind, gently turn your attention to a quality you like about yourself. Is there an ability or strength within yourself you can recognize? If still nothing comes to mind, reflect on the primal urge toward happiness within you, and the rightness and beauty of that.

In any of the above reflections, even if impatience or annoyance or fear should arise, don't be disheartened or anxious—see if you can return to the contemplation without guilt or judgment. The heart of skillful meditation is the ability to let go and begin again, over and over again. Even if you have to do that thousands of times during a session, it does not matter. There is no distance to traverse in recollecting our attention; as soon as we realize we have been lost in discursive thought, or have lost touch with our chosen contemplation, right in that very moment we can begin again. Nothing has been ruined, and there is no such thing as failing. There is nowhere the attention can wander to, and no duration of distraction, from which we cannot completely let go, in a moment, and begin again.

EXERCISE
Phrases of Lovingkindness

In doing metta practice, we gently repeat phrases that are meaningful in terms of what we wish, first for ourselves and then for others. We begin by befriending ourselves. The aspirations we articulate should be deeply felt and somewhat enduring (not something like "May I find a good show on television tonight"). Classically there are four phrases used:

> "May I be free from danger."
> "May I have mental happiness."
> "May I have physical happiness."
> "May I have ease of well-being."

I will describe these phrases here in detail, and you can experiment with them, alter them, or simply choose an alternative set of three or four phrases. Discover personally in your own heartfelt investigation what is truly significant for you.

"*May I be free from danger.*" We begin to extend care and lovingkindness toward ourselves with the wish that we may find freedom from danger, that we may know safety. We ultimately wish that all beings as well as ourselves have a sense of refuge, have a safe haven, have freedom from internal torment and external violence.

There is a nightmarish quality to life without safety. When we live repeatedly lost in conditioned states such as anger and greed, continually being hurt and hurting others—there is no peace or safety. When we are awakened at night by anxiety, guilt, and agitation—there is no peace or safety. When we live in a world of overt violence, which rests on the disempowerment of people and the loneliness of unspoken and silenced abuse—there is no peace or safety. This deep aspiration is the traditional beginning. "May I be free from danger." Other possible phrases are "May I have safety" and "May I be free from fear."

"*May I have mental happiness.*" If we were in touch with our own loveliness, if we felt less fearful of others, if we trusted our ability to love, we would have mental happiness. In the same vein, if we could relate skillfully to the torments of the mind that arise, and not nourish or cultivate them, we would have mental happiness. Even in very positive or fortunate circumstances, without mental happiness, we are miserable. Sometimes people use the phrase "May I be happy" or "May I be peaceful" or "May I be liberated."

"*May I have physical happiness.*" With this phrase we wish ourselves the enjoyment of health, freedom from physical pain, and harmony with our bodies. If freedom from pain is not a realistic possibility, we aspire to receive the pain with friendliness and patience, thereby not transforming physical pain into mental torment. You might also use a phrase such as "May I be healthy," "May I be healed," "May I make a friend of my body," or "May I embody my love and understanding."

"*May I have ease of well-being.*" This phrase points to the exigencies of everyday life—concerns such as relationships, family issues, and livelihood. With the expression of this phrase we wish that these elements of our day-to-day lives be free from struggle, that they be accomplished gracefully, and easily. Alternative phrases could be "May I live with ease" or "May lovingkindness manifest throughout my life" or "May I dwell in peace."

Sit comfortably. You can begin with five minutes of reflection on the good within you or your wish to be happy. Then choose three or four phrases that express what you most deeply wish for yourself, and repeat them over and over again. You can coordinate the phrases with the breath, if you wish, or simply have your mind rest in the phrases without a physical anchor. Feel free to experiment, and be creative. Without trying to force or demand a loving feeling, see if there are circumstances you can imagine yourself in where you can more readily experience friendship with yourself. Is it seeing yourself as a young child? One friend imagined himself sitting surrounded by all the most loving people he had ever heard of in the world, receiving their kindness and good wishes. For the first time, love for himself seemed to enter his heart.

Develop a gentle pacing with the phrases; there is no need to rush through them, or say them harshly. You are offering yourself a gift with each phrase. If your attention wanders, or if difficult feelings or memories arise, try to let go of them in the spirit of kindness, and begin again repeating the metta phrases:

"May I be free from danger."
"May I have mental happiness."
"May I have physical happiness."
"May I have ease of well-being."

There are times when feelings of unworthiness come up strongly, and you clearly see the conditions that limit your love for yourself. Breathe gently, accept that these feelings have arisen, remember the beauty of your wish to be happy, and return to the metta phrases.

3

Facets of Lovingkindness

*A pearl goes up for auction. No one has enough,
so the pearl buys itself.*
                                     —*Rumi*

LOVE EXISTS IN ITSELF, not relying on owning or being owned. Like the pearl, love can only buy itself, because love is not a matter of currency or exchange. No one has enough to buy it, but everyone has enough to cultivate it. Metta reunites us with what it means to be alive and unbound.

Researchers once gave a plant to every resident of a nursing home. Half of these elderly people were told that the plants were theirs to care for—that they had to pay close attention to their plants' needs for water and sunlight, and should respond carefully to those needs. The other half of the residents were told that the plants were theirs to enjoy but that they did not have to take any responsibility for them; the nursing staff would care for the plants. At the end of a year, the researchers compared the two groups of elders. The residents who had been asked to care for their plants were living considerably longer than the norm, were much healthier, and were more oriented toward and connected to their world. The other residents, those who had plants but did not have to stay responsive to them, simply reflected the norms for people their age in longevity, health, alertness, and engagement with the world.

This study suggests, among other things, the enlivening power of connection, of love, of intimacy. This is the effect that metta can have on our lives. But when I heard about the study, I also reflected on how often we regard intimacy as a force between ourselves and something outside ourselves—another person, a pet, or even a plant—and how rarely we consider the force of being intimate *with ourselves*, with our own inner experience. How rarely do we lay claim to our own lives and feel connected to ourselves!

A way to discover intimacy with ourselves and all of life is to live with integrity, basing our lives on a vision of compassionate nonharming. When we dedicate ourselves to actions that do not hurt ourselves or others, our lives become all of a piece, a seamless garment with nothing separate or disconnected in the spiritual reality we discover.

In order to live with integrity, we must stop fragmenting and compartmentalizing our lives. Telling lies at work and then expecting great truths in meditation is nonsensical. Using our sexual energy in a way that harms ourselves or others, and then expecting to know transcendent love in another arena, is mindless. Every aspect of our lives is connected to every other aspect of our lives. This truth is the basis for an awakened life.

When we live with integrity, we further enhance intimacy with ourselves by being able to rejoice, taking active delight in our actions. Rejoicing opens us tremendously, dissolving our barriers, thereby enabling intimacy to extend to all of life. Joy has so much capacity to eliminate separation that the Buddha said, "Rapture is the gateway to nirvana."

The enlivening force itself is rapture. It brightens our vitality, our gratitude, and our love. We begin to develop rapture by rejoicing in our own goodness. We reflect on the good things we have done, recollecting times when we have been generous, or times when we have been caring. Perhaps we can think of a time when it would have been easy to hurt somebody, or to tell a lie, or to be dismissive, yet we made the effort not to do that. Perhaps we can think of a time when we gave something up in a way that freed our mind and helped someone else. Or perhaps we can think of a time when we have overcome some fear and reached out to someone. These reflections open us to a wellspring of happiness that may have been hidden from us before.

Contemplating the goodness within ourselves is a classical

meditation, done to bring light, joy, and rapture to the mind. In contemporary times this practice might be considered rather embarrassing, because so often the emphasis is on all the unfortunate things we have done, all the disturbing mistakes we have made. Yet this classical reflection is not a way of increasing conceit. It is rather a commitment to our own happiness, seeing our happiness as the basis for intimacy with all of life. It fills us with joy and love for ourselves and a great deal of self-respect.

Significantly, when we do metta practice, we begin by directing metta toward ourselves. This is the essential foundation for being able to offer genuine love to others. When we truly love ourselves, we want to take care of others, because that is what is most enriching, or nourishing, for us. When we have a genuine inner life, we are intimate with ourselves and intimate with others. The insight into our inner world allows us to connect to everything around us, so that we can see quite clearly the oneness of all that lives. We see that all beings want to be happy, and that this impulse unites us. We can recognize the rightness and beauty of our common urge toward happiness, and realize intimacy in this shared urge.

If we are practicing metta and we cannot see the goodness in ourselves or in someone else, then we reflect on the fundamental wish to be happy that underlies all action. "Just as I want to be happy, all beings want to be happy." This reflection gives rise to openness, awareness, and love. As we commit to these values, we become embodiments of a lineage that stretches back through beginningless time. All good people of all time have wanted to express openness, awareness, and love. With every phrase of metta, we are declaring our alignment with these values.

From this beginning, metta practice proceeds in a very structured and specific way. After we have spent some time directing metta to ourselves, we then move on to someone who has been very good to us, for whom we feel gratitude and respect. In the traditional terminology, this person is known as a "benefactor." Later we move to someone who is a beloved friend. It is relatively easy to direct lovingkindness to these categories of beings. (We say "beings" rather than "people" to allow the possibility of including animals in these categories.) After we have established this state of connection, we move on to those toward whom it may be harder to direct lovingkindness. In this way we challenge our limits and extend our capacity for benevolence.

Thus, we next direct lovingkindness to someone toward whom we feel neutral, someone for whom we feel neither great liking nor disliking. This is often an interesting time in the practice, because it may be difficult to find somebody for whom we have no instantaneous judgment. If we can find such a neutral person, we direct metta toward them.

After this, we are ready for the next step: directing metta toward someone with whom we have experienced conflict, someone toward whom we feel lack of forgiveness, or anger, or fear. In the Buddhist scriptures this person is somewhat dramatically known as "the enemy." This is a very powerful stage in the practice, because the enemy, or the person with whom we have difficulty, stands right at the division between the finite and the infinite radiance of love. At this point, conditional love unfolds into unconditional love. Here dependent love can turn to the flowering of an independent love that is not based upon getting what we want or having our expectations met. Here we learn that the inherent happiness of love is not compromised by likes and dislikes, and thus, like the sun, it can shine on everything. This love is truly boundless. It is born out of freedom, and it is offered freely.

Through the power of this practice, we cultivate an equality of loving feeling toward ourselves and all beings. There was a time in Burma when I was practicing metta intensively. I had taken about six weeks to go through all the different categories: myself, benefactor, friend, neutral person, and enemy. After I had spent these six weeks doing the metta meditation all day long, my teacher, U Pandita, called me into his room and said, "Suppose you were walking in the forest with your benefactor, your friend, your neutral person, and your enemy. Bandits come up and demand that you choose one person in your group to be sacrificed. Which one would you choose to die?"

I was shocked at U Pandita's question. I sat there and looked deep into my heart, trying to find a basis from which I could choose. I saw that I could not feel any distinction between any of those people, including myself. Finally I looked at U Pandita and replied, "I couldn't choose; everyone seems the same to me."

U Pandita then asked, "You wouldn't choose your enemy?" I thought a minute and then answered, "No, I couldn't."

Finally U Pandita asked me, "Don't you think you should be able to sacrifice yourself to save the others?" He asked the question as if more than anything else in the world he wanted me to say, "Yes, I'd sacrifice myself." A lot of conditioning rose up in me—an urge to please him, to be "right," to win approval. But there was no way I could honestly say yes, so I said, "No, I can't see any difference between myself and any of the others." He simply nodded in response, and I left.

Later I was reading the *Visuddhi Magga*, one of the great commentarial works of Buddhist literature, which describes different meditation techniques and the experiences of practicing them. In the section on metta meditation, I came to that very question about the bandits. The answer I had given was indeed considered the correct one for the intensive practice of metta.

Of course, in different life situations, many different courses of action might be appropriate. But the point here is that metta does not mean that we denigrate ourselves in *any* situation in order to uphold other people's happiness. Authentic intimacy is not brought about by denying our own desire to be happy in unhappy deference to others, nor by denying others in narcissistic deference to ourselves. Metta means equality, oneness, wholeness. To truly walk the Middle Way of the Buddha, to avoid the extremes of addiction and self-hatred, we must walk in friendship with ourselves as well as with all beings.

When we have insight into our inner world and what brings us happiness, then wordlessly, intuitively, we understand others. As though there were no longer a barrier defining the boundaries of our caring, we can feel close to others' experience of life. We see that when we are angry, there is an element of pain in the anger that is not different from the pain that others feel when they are angry. When we feel love, there is a distinct and special joy in that feeling. We come to know that this is the nature of love itself, and that other beings filled with love experience this same joy.

In practicing metta we do not have to make a certain feeling happen. In fact, during the practice we see that we feel differently at different times. Any momentary emotional tone is far less relevant than the considerable power of intention we harness as we say these phrases. As we repeat, "May I be happy; may all beings be happy," we are planting seeds by forming this powerful intention in the mind. The seed will bear fruit in its own time.

When I was practicing metta intensively in Burma, at times when I repeated the phrases, I would picture myself in a wide-open field planting seeds. Doing metta, we plant the seeds of love, knowing that nature will take its course and in time those seeds will bear fruit. Some seeds will come to fruition quickly, some slowly, but our work is simply to plant the seeds. Every time we form the intention in the mind for our own happiness or for the happiness of others, we are doing our work; we are channeling the powerful energies of our own minds. Beyond that, we can trust the laws of nature to continually support the flowering of our love. As Pablo Neruda says:

> Perhaps the earth can teach us
> as when everything seems dead
> and later proves to be alive.

When we started our retreat center, Insight Meditation Society, in 1975, many of us there decided to do a self-retreat for a month to inaugurate the center. I planned to do metta for the entire month. This was before I'd been to Burma, and it would be my first opportunity to do intensive and systematic metta meditation. I had heard how it was done in extended practice, and I planned to follow that schedule. So the first week I spent directing lovingkindness toward myself. I felt absolutely nothing. It was the dreariest, most boring week I had known in some time. I sat there saying, "May I be happy, may I be peaceful," over and over again with no obvious result.

Then, as it happened, someone we knew in the community had a problem, and a few of us had to leave the retreat suddenly. I felt even worse, thinking, "Not only did I spend this week doing metta and getting nothing from it, but I also never even got beyond directing metta toward myself. So on top of everything else, I was really selfish."

I was in a frenzy getting ready to leave. As I was hurriedly getting everything together in my bathroom, I dropped a jar. It shattered all over the floor. I still remember my immediate response: "You are really a klutz, but I love you." And then I thought, "Wow! Look at that. Something did happen in this week of practice."

So the intention is enough. We form the *intention* in our mind for our happiness and the happiness of all. This is different from struggling to fabricate a certain feeling, to create it out of our will, to make it happen. We just settle back and plant the seeds without worrying about the immediate result. That is our work. If we do our work, then manifold benefits will surely come.

Fortunately, the Buddha was characteristically precise about what those benefits include. He said that the intimacy and caring that fill our hearts as the force of lovingkindness develops will bring eleven particular advantages:

1. You will sleep easily.
2. You will wake easily.
3. You will have pleasant dreams.
4. People will love you.
5. Devas [celestial beings] and animals will love you.
6. Devas will protect you.
7. External dangers [poisons, weapons, and fire] will not harm you.
8. Your face will be radiant.
9. Your mind will be serene.
10. You will die unconfused.
11. You will be reborn in happy realms.

People doing formal metta practice often memorize these eleven benefits and recite them to themselves regularly. Reminding ourselves of the fruit of our intention and effort can bring a lot of faith and rapture, sustaining us through those inevitable times when it seems as if the practice is not "getting anywhere." When we consider each of these benefits, we can see more fully how metta revolutionizes our lives.

When we steep our hearts in lovingkindness, we are able to sleep easily, to awaken easily, and to have pleasant dreams. To have self-respect in life, to walk through this life with grace and confidence, means having a commitment to nonharming and to loving care. If we do not have these things, we can neither rest nor be at peace; we are always fighting against ourselves. The feelings we create by harming are painful both for ourselves and for others. Thus harming leads to guilt, tension, and complexity. But living a clear and simple life, free from resentment, fear, and guilt, extends into our sleeping, dreaming, and waking.

The next benefit the Buddha pointed out is that if we practice metta we will receive in return the love of others. This is not a heartless, calculating motivation, but rather a recognition that the energy we extend in this world draws to it that same kind of energy. If we extend the force of love, love returns to us. The American psychologist William James once said, "My experience is what I agree to attend to. Only those items I notice shape my mind." Perhaps this is partially how this law works—opening to the energy of love within us, we can notice it more specifically around us.

It happens on other levels as well. If we are committed in our lives to the force of lovingkindness, then people know that they can trust us. They know we will not deceive them; we will not harm them. By being a beacon of trustworthiness in this world, we become a safe haven for others and a good friend.

The next set of benefits the Buddha points out promises that if we practice metta we will be protected. Devas and other invisible beings are classically taught as part of the Buddhist cosmology, but we don't have to believe in the intervention of invisible forces in order to comprehend how the practice of metta protects us. This assertion does not mean being protected in the sense that nothing bad will ever happen to us, because clearly the vicissitudes of life are completely outside our control. Pleasure and pain, gain and loss, praise and blame, and fame and ill repute will revolve throughout our lives. But nevertheless we can be protected by the nature of how we receive, how we hold that which our lives bring us.

Albert Einstein said, "The splitting of the atom has changed everything except for how we think." How we think, how we look at our lives, is all-important, and the degree of love we manifest determines the degree of spaciousness and freedom we can bring to life's events.

Imagine taking a very small glass of water and putting into it a teaspoon of salt. Because of the small size of the container, the teaspoon of salt is going to have a big impact upon the water. However, if you approach a much larger body of water, such as a lake, and put into it that same teaspoonful of salt, it will not have the same intensity of impact, because of the vastness and openness of the vessel receiving it. Even when the salt remains the same, the spaciousness of the vessel receiving it changes everything.

We spend a lot of our lives looking for a feeling of safety or protection; we try to alter the amount of salt that comes our way. Ironically, the salt is the very thing that we cannot do anything about, as life changes and offers us repeated ups and downs. Our true work is to create a container so immense that any amount of salt, even a truckload, can come into it without affecting our capacity to receive it. No situation, even an extreme one, then can mandate a particular reaction.

Once I had a meditation student who had been a child in Nazi-occupied Europe. She recounted an instance when she was around ten years old when a German soldier held a gun to her chest—a situation that would readily arouse terror. Yet she related feeling no fear at all, thinking, "You may be able to kill my body, but you can't kill me." What a spacious reaction! It is in this way that lovingkindness opens the vastness of mind in us, which is ultimately our greatest protection.

Another benefit of cultivating metta is that one's face becomes very clear and shining. This means that an unfeigned inner beauty shines forth. We know in life situations how mind affects matter, how if we are enraged about something, it shows in our face. If somebody is full of hatred, it shows in the way they stand, the way they move, the way their jaw is set. It is not very attractive. No amount of makeup, jewelry, or embellishments bring beauty to a sullen, disgruntled, angry face. In just the same way, when someone's mind is filled with the rapture of lovingkindness or compassion, it is beautiful to see the expression of light, of radiance, on their face and bearing.

With the practice of metta, one also has a serene mind. The feeling of lovingkindness generates great peace. This is the mind that can say, "You are really a klutz, but I love you." It is a feeling endowed with acceptance, patience, and spaciousness. This great peace allows union with all of life, because we are not relying on changing circumstances for our happiness.

The peace of metta offers the kind of happiness that gives us the ability to concentrate. Serenity is the most important ingredient in being able to be present or being able to concentrate the mind. Concentration is an act of cherishing a chosen object. If we have no serenity, the mind will be scattered, and we will not be able to gather in the energy that is being lost to distraction. When we can concentrate, all of this energy is returned to us. This is the potency that heals us.

If we practice metta, another major benefit is that we will die unconfused. Our habitual ways of thinking, acting, and relating to life tend to be the ones that are strongest at the time of death as well. If we spend a lifetime feeling separate and apart, cultivating anger, giving way to frustration, to fear, to desire, that will likely be the mental-emotional environment within which we face our death. But if we have lived our life in a way that honors our connectedness, reflects our oneness, and cultivates caring and giving, that is likely to be how we will die.

The last specific benefit the Buddha spoke of was being reborn in happy realms as a result of filling our hearts with lovingkindness. The potential for rebirth again and again in various realms of pleasure or pain is part of the Buddhist worldview. For someone who subscribes to this vision of life, rebirth in a realm where one can attain liberation is most important. For those who don't subscribe to this vision, the benefits of metta can surely be seen to come to us in *this* lifetime.

Metta is a priceless treasure that enlivens us and brings us into intimacy with ourselves and others. It is the force of love that will lead beyond fragmentation, loneliness, and fear. The late Hindu guru Neem Karoli Baba often said, "Don't throw anyone out of your heart." One of the most powerful healings (and greatest adventures) of our lifetime can come about as we learn to live by this dictum.

EXERCISE
The Benefits of Lovingkindness

You can begin by reflecting on the benefits of doing metta meditation, confident that in time they will certainly accrue. The various benefits are born out of increasing self-respect and respect for others, kindness, and living in harmony. You can recite the traditional list if you wish, or parts of it, or create a list generated out of your own certainty in the power of love. Remember that this reflection is done to bring us joy and confidence: we are gifted with an urge to be happy *and* an understanding of a path to happiness. If we walk this path, it will result in great benefit simply and naturally.

EXERCISE
The Benefactor

Spend a few minutes contemplating the goodness within you, or the rightness of your wish to be happy. Then gently repeat the metta phrases you have chosen, offering friendship to yourself. After about ten minutes, see if you can call to mind someone for whom you feel strong respect or gratitude. This is the person known in the Buddhist texts as the benefactor. Traditionally, it is taught that if the benefactor you choose is still alive, it will deepen the level of concentration you can attain. It is also recommended that this person not be someone you feel sexual desire for, since it is important at this stage to be able to distinguish the feeling of metta from the feeling of desire.

Call this person to mind, perhaps visualizing them, or saying their name to yourself. Recall the different ways they have helped you, or contributed to you or to the world, and the goodness within them. If rapture should arise, allow it to energize you. If it doesn't arise, don't seek it—simply contemplate the benefactor and their goodness, or their wish to be happy. Then direct the metta phrases toward your benefactor, enveloping the person with lovingkindness. Whether or not a feeling of love arises, you can stay connected to the phrases, their meaning, and a sense of the benefactor. Your choice of benefactor may change over time, which is fine.

It is best to start out using the same phrases you have directed toward yourself, to begin to break down the barriers between self and other: "Just as I want to be happy, so do you want to be happy. May you be happy." If over time the phrases modulate to fit the particular being, that is fine.

We say the phrases as though cherishing a fragile, precious object in our hand. Were we to grab on to it too tightly, it would shatter and break. Were we to be lax and negligent, it would fall out of our hand and break. We cherish the object gently, carefully, without force but paying close attention. Try to connect to each phrase, one at a time. There is no need to worry about what has gone by or to anticipate what has not yet come, not even the next phrase. Don't struggle to manufacture a feeling of love. Simply repeat the phrases, thereby planting the potent seeds of intention, and trust that nature will take its own course.

4
Hindrances to Lovingkindness
Desire and Attachment

> Where love rules, there is no will to power; and where power predominates, there love is lacking. The one is the shadow of the other.
>
> — *Carl Jung*

ONE YEAR, when I went to teach meditation in the Soviet Union, I happened to arrive exactly the day before the attempt to remove then-President Mikhail Gorbachev from power. When the coup began, there was, of course, tremendous fear and chaos. I went to the American embassy to register, hoping to get some guidance on what to do. The embassy was a riot of turbulence and desperation. Soviet citizens as well as Americans were crying out for help. "Please let me see the consul!" one woman kept repeating. "My nephew's papers just came through yesterday. You must let him emigrate, I beg you!" Americans involved in joint business ventures with Soviet citizens were also there, frightened at the prospect of losing a great deal of money. Many waited, shocked and worried, facing the possibility of losing their deeply cherished dreams.

In the midst of this frenzy, I found myself standing alongside an American tour group leader who was asking embassy personnel for advice on how to handle the crisis. Given the volatile nature of the populace, the only thing the man he spoke with could offer was the suggestion to stay out of crowds. In shock and dismay, the tour group leader looked up and asked, "Does that mean I can't go shopping?!"

Desire—grasping, clinging, greed, attachment—is a state of mind that defines what we think we need in order to be happy. We project all of our hopes and dreams of fulfillment onto some object of our attention. This may be a certain activity or outcome, a particular thing or person. Deluded by our temporary enchantment, we view the world with tunnel vision. That object, and that alone, will make us happy. Who has not been greatly infatuated with some idea or some person, only to look again two months later, six months later, a year later, and think, "What was that all about?"

Buddhist texts liken desire in the mind to a pond that has been filled with dye. We no longer can see to the bottom of the pond. Our vision is obscured. In contrast to metta, the force of love that melts barriers and enhances the natural luminosity of the mind, desire generates divisiveness and clouds the mind with clinging and attachment. For this reason, desire is considered one of the hindrances to metta.

To explore desire is to explore the question, "What is it I really want and need in order to be happy?" Feelings of desire are quite natural, but when we follow them to find our happiness, we must be aware of their potential dangers. In an effort to fulfill desires, we may hurt someone, or ourselves. We may become dependent on having certain objects of our desire and on their remaining exactly the same. We may very well think the satisfaction of a desire will give us something that in fact it will not and cannot give.

We may forsake a lot, or make many compromises in order to obtain the objects of our desire. We continually give up things in order to get something else, perhaps something more remote or elusive. Our desires delude us, as we lose sight of what we actually do have, in an effort to obtain what we do not have. What we end up with is a continual sense of loss. One of our main losses is contentment.

As a result of desire, we may also lose connection to others. We are competing for happiness as though it could be contained in a limited object, person, or experience. We define the object of our desire as very limited in supply, and our happiness as entirely dependent upon obtaining it. We resent people or things that seem to obstruct the fulfillment of that desire. We feel envy and jealousy. These are actually very isolating feelings. With attachment, all that seems to exist is just me and that object I desire.

We can lose not only our feelings of connection to others but also compassion for them. Some years ago a friend invested some money in the stock market. Soon after, the market began falling sharply. My friend spent weeks avidly listening to the news and reading the paper, closely following how particular world events might affect his stock. He found himself responding to news of war, famine, and calamity with the immediate concern: "I wonder if this will help my stock?" Fortunately he ended up selling his stocks and could once more enjoy his freedom from greed and his connection to others.

When the source of satisfaction or happiness is seen as limited, we fix upon it. Such attachment restricts us not only by narrowly defining what we want, but also by narrowly defining what we think is possible for us.

I have always been grateful that when I first went to India in the early seventies, I did not arrive with a long list of requirements for my well-being, like hot running water or certain types of food. If I had had such a list, I could never have stayed to experience the most significant events of my life. Thwarted by my desires, I would have been unable to take risks. Attachment to what we think we must have in order to be happy can contract our lives. We mainly live our lives in this deluded mode of having. That is the essence of desire and attachment. It is driven by acquisitiveness. We have material objects. We have people. We say, "I have a husband," "I have a friend," "I have children."

The same spirit of acquisition applies in relation to information or belief systems. We have views and opinions that define us. Thus our world is split into divergent camps defined by nationalism, ethnicity, and fundamentalist doctrines.

We even regard our own bodies and minds as things to possess. We lay claim to our bodies as though they were not subject to change. We lay claim to our minds as though we should be able to control what arises within them. The body and the mind are "ours." Yet this body has the audacity to give up, to die. Life in this sense is looked upon as an object that I can keep or lose; but if we consider carefully, is this right? If we try to hold on to our lives, the holding on takes precedence over the quality of our lives. And this mind simply will not obey us. We tell it to feel one thing, and it feels another; to think one thing, and it thinks another. Yet "having" something makes us think we can control it.

I once received as a housewarming present a very simple glass teakettle, which I liked a lot; it became one of my favorite possessions. One day I had some water for tea boiling in that kettle on the stove. When I went to pick the kettle up, it shattered into many pieces, splashing the boiling water over my hand and burning me. My primary response when this happened was a feeling of betrayal. This teapot had betrayed me. I thought, "I liked it so much. It was one of my very favorite things. How could it do that?"

When we think of ourselves as possessing people, the desire to control them and the consequent feelings of betrayal can be especially strong. We tend to watch them carefully all of the time to see what they might next do. This vigilance born of anxiety creates a lot of tension. If we think we own someone, if we "have" them, we posit an "us" and "them." That in itself is a source of separation. We actually create a gulf between the possessor and the possessed. The more we sense separation between ourselves and them, the more we try to control them. We become more concerned with our ability to hold on to them than we are with enjoying our contact with them.

There are many ways in which we think of ourselves as possessing people. We may be in a healing or helping relationship with somebody. It is easy in that situation to expect people to respond in a certain way. "Why aren't you getting better?" From that perspective people often do not seem to behave correctly. We feel betrayed and resentful.

We tend to seek happiness, a sense of meaning, and a sense of purpose by acquiring and then preserving certain objects of desire from which, by definition, we are isolated because of the way we relate to them. The fulfillment we have in owning, in desiring, is temporary and illusory, because there is nothing at all we can have that we will not lose eventually. And so there is always fear. We go round and round in circles, chasing after things, trying to have more and more and more, and then we die. Talk about betrayal!

The Buddha said, "Craving brings anxiety and fear." Actually, craving and fear circle around each other. Fear can often give rise to an intensified attachment, because if we fear that something might be taken away, we will crave for a means to secure it. By its very nature, desire brings fear, because we look to an unstable, changing world to bring us stable happiness. Thus we stand on quicksand, compounding the problem by blaming ourselves for failing to find security in this frantic and illusory pursuit.

Attachment, which is based on desire, is called in the Buddhist teaching the root of suffering because of its two accompanying qualities: seeking and guarding. Seeking is endless. It never comes to a state of rest; it never ceases. Guarding involves trying to hold on, and this creates fear and anxiety, because everything we can know with this body and mind is in constant change.

When I first began meditation practice, after the difficulties in the beginning, I went through a period when as I sat I experienced lovely, floating sensations in my body and serene, peaceful mind states. Immediately I started thinking, "Won't it be wonderful to spend the entire rest of my life in just this state?" I would imagine myself five or ten years hence, floating down the streets of New York, wearing a beatific smile, having exactly the same experience I was having at that moment.

But of course it never lasted. In no more than twenty minutes, my legs would start aching or I would become sleepy or restless. Every time this happened, I would blame myself for the change: "What did I do wrong to make my nice feelings go away?" But they did not go away because I had done anything wrong; they went away simply because everything changes. There is no way we can stop this flow of change and successfully cling to pleasant experience.

However, when we see the world through the eyes of desire, we are always hoping that it will somehow magically provide us only good things; there will be no bad things, no painful things. Although the world actually *is* magically providing, that does not mean there is no pain. Pain is not a sign of things gone wrong. Our lives are actually a constant succession of pleasure and pain, getting what we want, then losing it. We experience pleasure and pain, gain and loss, praise and blame, fame and disrepute, constantly changing out of our control. This is what the world is naturally providing, and still we can be happy.

What is it that we need in order to be happy? Do we really need what the world tells us we do? Often what we think we need in order to be happy is somebody else's construction of reality. "Samsara," the name of a French perfume, is a good example of such a construction. In the Pali and Sanskrit languages of classical Buddhism, *samsara* means this world of constant change, the cycle of birth and death, of suffering. But advertising for this perfume proclaims Samsara as "subtle yet lingering, a timeless fulfillment." Just what we all want. Is it really a timeless fulfillment, at last?

We may think that we want a lot of money in order to be happy, but it's not that we want a lot of pieces of paper with pictures of presidents on them piled up everywhere, or even a lot of objects that they could purchase. What we really want is what having a lot of money implies to us. It may imply security or power. It may imply an ability to make choices, or it may imply having time to play.

If we look very carefully, we realize that after our basic needs have been met, what we really want are certain mind states. In fact, when we talk about having a lot of money, we are really talking about mind states such as security or power or freedom. Even when people have a lot of money, they may not have these mind states. They may not feel very powerful or secure.

We discover when we see reality accurately that mind states are actually a function of our *being*; they are not a function of how much we have or what we have. This is one of the ironies of desire. There are so many things that we can have, and that we do have, without the suffering of attachment, without compromise or loss. These are inner qualities such as love, faith, wisdom, and peace. Such states are not produced by a process of having more and more, through feverish seeking.

When we become lost in desire, we are put firmly into the

framework of linear time. We become focused on getting what we do not yet have, or on keeping what we do have. We become oriented toward the future. To be caught in this concept of linear time brings us to what in Buddhist teachings is called *bhava*, or becoming, always falling into the next moment. It is as if before each breath ends, we are leaning forward to grasp at the next breath.

If we walked around all the time with our bodies leaning forward, can you imagine the kind of aching we would experience? Our backs, our necks, our legs would really hurt. In just that same way, our hearts really hurt because we are thrust forward all of the time, in wanting, in seeking, in leaning into things, in being dependent on particular things or people or even beliefs for our happiness. We have one impermanent experience, and, unable to be at peace as it passes, we reach out and grab for another.

The Tibetan Buddhist tradition defines renunciation as accepting what comes into our lives and letting go of what leaves our lives. To renounce in this sense is to come to a state of simple being. We have a moment of seeing, a moment of hearing, tasting, touching, smelling, thinking—just a moment, and then it is gone. When we look very carefully, we see that our experience is like a cascade of impressions. If we rely upon any one of these transiencies for a sense of permanent satisfaction, we lose the happiness of simply being. Just imagine for a moment the stillness and peace of not leaning forward even for the next breath. This is *being*, rather than *becoming*, and this is the power and fullness of metta.

Metta occurs in timelessness. With real love we do not focus on the future—on what we want, or what we fear, or what we have to guard against. We can actually allow things to be the way they are. Metta takes us outside the realm of time, expectation, and disappointment.

Metta does not depend upon striking a bargain or setting up an exchange. Desire says, "I will love you, I will take care of you, I will offer you this or that, as long as you meet my expectations and satisfy my needs." The loving feelings that we have in such bargaining are limited to those we like, because they give us what we want. We love someone, and then when they disappoint us, we no longer love them. This kind of limited love is based upon desire and attachment.

We can think we're feeling metta for someone when we're really feeling attachment and desire. For this reason, desire is called the "near enemy" of metta. Because it can feel so similar, it can masquerade as metta—until it reaches its limit. But metta is boundless. It is open and freely given. Metta does not create a duality between subject and object; it does not try to control or hold on; it is not subject to the same fears and frailties of betrayal. Metta is based on desirelessness.

Desirelessness—detachment—is not a cold, hard state in which we do not care what is going on. The opposite of attachment is not a sullen withdrawal from things or an attitude of indifference. It is very full, very alive, and very open. The energetic manifestation of desirelessness is love, which Mohandas Gandhi called "the most subtle force in the universe." It is subtle because it can go anywhere, like the wind—unlike clinging or attachment, which fixes on something and then cannot move or change. We come to desirelessness by purifying the mind of the force of craving. This can be done in several ways.

We purify the mind of the force of craving by not trying to control the uncontrollable. Once a friend's seven-year-old daughter woke up screaming in the middle of the night. My friend went to her and asked, "What's the matter? Did you have a bad dream?" Her daughter answered, "Yes, I dreamed that I was out in a garden because I was chasing the dog, and a gigantic swarm of bees surrounded me, and then I died."

My friend was incredulous. "You actually died! I myself have dreamed of nearly dying, but never of actually dying. What was it like?" The child thought for a moment. "I suffered a lot, and then I stopped struggling, and it was all right."

We must understand the nature of our struggle, and how to make our experience of life and death all right. To relinquish the futile effort to control change is one of the strengthening forces of true detachment, and thus true love.

We purify the mind of craving by practicing generosity. Desire, greed, is a centripetal longing in which we seek to draw everything inward toward ourselves. Giving is a basic reorientation of that attitude into one of opening, one of offering. Generosity is not merely the overt action of giving somebody something material; it can also be giving of care, of protection, of kindness, and of love. Generosity is not just interpersonal; it is also an inward state, a generosity of the spirit that extends to ourselves as well as to others.

We also purify the mind of the force of grasping by developing gratitude. Instead of walking around with the feeling that we do not have enough, that there is never enough, that we are not enough, we can recognize that the world is in fact magically providing, with just what it is providing.

We purify the mind of the force of craving through the power of simplifying, knowing what we need in order to be happy. True happiness cannot be found in some thing or some person, because as everything changes, that level of happiness is bound to be temporary. More enduring is the possibility of experiencing a loving heart in any circumstance.

To live without attachment or desire means being at one with our own lives in the most natural, spontaneous way. When His Holiness the Dalai Lama won the Nobel Peace Prize, someone commented that to give the Dalai Lama a peace prize was like giving Mother Nature an art award. For all of us, love can be the natural state of our own being; naturally at peace, naturally connected, because this becomes the reflection of who we simply are.

EXERCISE
Reflection on Happiness

It is quite useful to sincerely explore the question, "What do I truly need in order to be happy?" Let your mind roam freely over thoughts, memories, and desires. Hold all possibilities in the context of this question, not seeking to reject or exclude anything, but remaining honest throughout. Remember that conditional and fleeting happiness is not our highest potential. Remember that if an object, person, or situation must change, it is futile to seek unchanging happiness there.

"What do I truly need in order to be happy?" Some guidance comes from a poem by Ryokan:

If we gain something, it was there from the beginning.
If we lose anything, it is hidden nearby.

EXERCISE

The Meaning of Friends

Think about what friendship means to you, what you value most in a friend and what you would most like to offer others as a friend. Are there qualities of trust, candor, fairness, or humor that stand out as being most important to you? What kind of person would you be able to turn to if you were in need? What does it mean to you to feel "at home" with someone? What would you like others to value in you as their friend?

Sometimes we are afraid to contemplate an action if it seems we will have to do it all alone; but if we can count on the presence of even one friend, there is less fear. This is the meaning of solidarity and the power of community. If we keep "wise company," as the Buddha said, and have good friends, we have one of the greatest resources for happiness and freedom.

EXERCISE

The Beloved Friend

Begin with a reflection on the benefits of metta, and the meaning of friendship to you. Then direct lovingkindness toward yourself for a few minutes. Next, call to mind someone you consider a good friend, saying their name, or maintaining an image of them, or getting a feeling of their presence. Once again the traditional teachings encourage beginning with someone who is still alive and who is not an object of sexual desire.

You can contemplate a likable quality or attribute of your friend, and take delight in their urge to be happy. Direct the force of lovingkindness toward them by repeating the metta phrases you have chosen for yourself, encompassing them in the field of your caring. If a different friend comes to mind, allow them to become the object of attention. If your mind wanders off into stories or plans, gently return to the repetition of the phrases. Use the same phrases you have used for yourself unless they change naturally, without contrivance or thought.

EXERCISE
The Neutral Person

Direct metta toward yourself, then someone for whom you have a feeling of lovingkindness—either your benefactor or your friend. Then see if you can call a neutral person to mind. As I mentioned before, it can be somewhat difficult to find someone for whom you have not formed an instant liking or disliking. It is helpful to choose someone whom you tend to see occasionally, since that will bring them, and your changing feelings for them, into clearer focus.

If you can think of a neutral person, directing metta toward them may actually be something of a relief, since you will have no intense feelings about this person to interfere with the practice. He or she is a generic living being, wanting to be happy just as all of us do, making mistakes just as all of us do. We have no reason to feel separate from this person or to begrudge their happiness.

Reflect on the neutral person's wish to be happy, identical to your own, and direct the metta phrases toward them:

"May you be free from danger."
"May you have mental happiness."
"May you have physical happiness."
"May you have ease of well-being."

If physical pain arises as you sit, quietly shift posture. Stay as comfortable as you can. If you feel bored, go back to sending metta to yourself, or to someone you care about deeply, then return to the neutral person.

Over time, it is common to discover an increase of caring and warmth toward the neutral person, as they seem closer and closer to you. They are, after all, a kind of nonerotic secret love. Once I returned to Barre after a metta course was held there, and was meeting our bookkeeper, who had sat that retreat. We were discussing someone we barely knew, who worked at the bank, and her face lit up as though she were in love. Startled, I questioned her, and she replied, "Oh, he was my neutral person during the metta retreat." I have seen this happen many times, in my own experience and in that of others, where the force of concentrating loving energy on someone opens a special place in our hearts for them, even if we never say a word to them!

5

Working with Anger and Aversion

Hatred can never cease by hatred.
Hatred can only cease by love.
This is an eternal law.

—*The Buddha*

WHEN I FIRST PRACTICED meditation with Sayadaw U Pandita, in 1984, I went through a period of disturbing memories about all the terrible things I had ever done. Memories of spurning childhood friends, of telling lies from seemingly good motives, of holding on to things when I was perfectly capable of giving them up, all came up to haunt me. I did not even want to tell the Sayadaw that I was experiencing this, but I did. I said, "You know, I just keep thinking of event after event after event—all of these bad things I've done. I feel terrible. I feel horrible. I feel awful."

U Pandita looked at me and asked, "Well, are you finally seeing the truth about yourself?" I was shocked at his response. Even though I was enveloped in self-judgment and criticism, something in his comment made me want to challenge it. I thought to myself, "No, I'm not seeing the truth about myself." And then he simply said, "Stop thinking about it." Only later would I understand the wisdom of his advice. Who among us has not done things to hurt people or to harm other creatures, or the earth itself? Through actions born of the mind state of aversion, we harm others and we harm ourselves. We experience aversion through a host of afflictions—anger, fear, guilt, impatience, grief, disappointment, dejection, anxiety, despair. Because hatred and aversion are the opposite of the state of love, they are considered the "far enemy" of metta.

The near enemy of metta, desire, is a subtler hindrance because it brings us temporary satisfaction. These states of aversion, by contrast, tear us apart; we burn when we are caught in them. The Buddha described the states of aversion as being of great consequence but easily overcome. They are of great consequence because they easily provoke strong action, leading us to perform unskillful deeds that hurt both ourselves and others. But even though such states are dangerous, nonetheless the pain of them is obvious, tangible, and easily felt. From beginning to end they bring great pain, so we are naturally moved to let them go.

The force of aversion manifests through us in two primary ways. One is outflowing, such as anger or rage. Such states have a lot of energy; they are powerful and expressive. We also experience aversion in a held-in way, as in grief, fear, disappointment, and despair. Here aversion's energy is frozen and paralyzing. Whether we are directing aversion toward ourselves or others, whether we are containing the aversion within our minds or expressing it toward others, these are the same mind states appearing in different forms.

One of the ways in which we direct aversion toward ourselves is in the form of guilt. As I experienced with Sayadaw U Pandita, as we go deeper in practice, we often begin spontaneously to review everything harmful we have ever done. These things just start coming up. People recall having disappointed a friend twenty-six years previously by not going to her sweet sixteen party, or the bitter retorts made to a partner no longer a part of their life. People suffer from having committed insurance fraud that remained undetected, or from the subtle, ongoing fear in a current friendship because of a lie told. It is very important to be able to acknowledge such things, to experience the pain, and then, as Sayadaw advised me, to just let them go—"stop thinking about it." Otherwise, we actually enhance a mistaken sense of self.

Buddhist psychology makes an interesting distinction between guilt and remorse. The feeling of guilt, or hatred directed toward oneself, lacerates. When we experience a strong feeling of guilt in the mind, we have little or no energy available for transformation or transcendence. We are defeated by the guilt itself, because it depletes us. We also feel very alone. Our thoughts focus on our worthlessness: "I'm the worst person in the world. Only I do these terrible things." However, such an attitude is actually very "self"-promoting. We become obsessed with "self" in the egotistical sense.

Remorse, by contrast, is a state of recognition. We realize that we have at some point done something or said something unskillful that caused pain, and we feel the pain of that recognition. But, crucially, remorse frees us to let go of the past. It leaves us with some energy to move on, resolved not to repeat our mistakes.

And guilt can be deceptive. We may feel that guilt can be a noble force to motivate us to serve others or perform wholesome actions. But guilt does not actually work in that way. When one is motivated by guilt or grief, one's own pain is center stage, just as when one is motivated by anger, one's outrage is center stage. When such feelings take the central role, we may lose consideration of what somebody else may actually need. There is not enough freedom from self-centeredness in our consciousness to see clearly, to be connected fully. Our own feelings overwhelm consciousness. We end up serving ourselves. How far this is from the invocation of Rabindranath Tagore: "Oh Lord, make me a better instrument through which you can blow."

Cultivating this mistaken concept of a permanent self also leads to aversion in the form of self-hatred or judgment. When we see the self as a fixed entity, we develop a strong habit of mind that drives our lives. If through our practice we can see the impersonal nature of the forces that arise and pass away, we experience a very different reality. For example, we can see anger, guilt, or grief arising in the mind as forces that come and go. Aversion is like a rainstorm, arising and passing away. It is not I, not me, not mine. It is not you or yours, either. In this recognition of emptiness, we look at other beings and see ourselves. Here is the birth of metta.

Self-hatred impedes this flowering of our practice. When the Dalai Lama visited Insight Meditation Society in 1979, somebody asked him, "I am a beginning meditation student and I feel quite worthless as a person. What can you say about that?" The Dalai

Lama replied, "You should never think like that; that is completely wrong thinking. You have the power of thought, and therefore the power of mind, and that is all you need." He was recognizing that we all have the potential for enlightenment, and therefore we should not denigrate that capacity by saying we are worthless.

We need to recollect this potential for awakening in order to see ourselves clearly. When we fall into aversion, we lose this perspective. I once approached my very first meditation teacher, S. N. Goenka, in an accusatory fashion and demanded to know, "Isn't there an easier way?" I was fed up and hated all my aches and pains. I think I actually thought he *did* know an easier way and was purposely withholding it from me so that I could suffer. It is quite amusing to look back on it, because he was a very compassionate person. After I asked that question, he just looked at me for a while. I fell into his eyes, which were radiant with a vastness of perspective, which never overlooked my capacity for freedom. From the point of view of a lifetime of spiritual endeavor, my sleepiness and knee pain did not seem so momentous and terrible. Whenever we forget the larger perspective, we become lost in the moment's little drama. Lost in aversion, we forget our capacity to love.

Once I received quite an angry letter from someone. It was one of those letters you would really rather not get, listing a lot of situations and circumstances that had happened. It basically said, "That was your fault, and that was your fault, and that was your fault, and *that* was your fault, too." It was not very pleasant. Throughout the rest of the day, I found myself composing responses in my mind to this letter. Mostly they ran along the lines of, "Well, actually, that's not my fault. It's your fault. And that was your fault, and that was your fault, and that was your fault, and *that* was your fault, too." I spent much of that day spinning it all out.

This kind of self-righteous anger solidifies into an almost choking sense of "I" and "other." Anger is such a grievous state because it means the death of the possibility of love or connection in that moment, in that situation. But what do we do when we feel anger or aversion?

There is a confusion in contemporary society about how to

relate to feelings of aversion. For example, it is difficult to understand the difference between *feeling* anger and *venting* anger. When we undertake a spiritual practice, it is important that we open to all that arises, that we recognize, acknowledge, and accept everything we feel. We have a long conditioning of self-deception, of keeping certain things outside the sphere of our awareness, of repressing them. Overcoming our denial and repression and opening to states of aversion can be very healing. But in the process, we may pay the price of becoming lost in anger if, through misunderstanding, we indulge it.

Most contemporary psychological research shows that when one expresses anger quite often in one's life, it leads to the easy expression of anger. Expressing anger becomes a habit. Many people assume that we have a certain amount of anger inside, and that if we do not want to keep it inside, we have to put it outside; somehow if it is outside, it is not going to be inside anymore. Anger seems like a solid thing. But, in fact, we discover, if we observe carefully, that anger has no solidity. In reality it is merely a conditioned response that arises and passes away. It is crucial for us to see that when we *identify* with these passing states as being solid and who we truly are, we let them rule us, and we are compelled to act in ways that cause harm to ourselves and others. Our opening needs to rest on a basis of *nonidentification*. Recognizing aversion or anger in the mind as transitory is very different from identifying with them as being who we really are, and then acting on them.

Anger is a very complex emotion, with a lot of different components. There are strands of disappointment, fear, sadness, all woven together. If the emotions and thoughts are taken as a whole, anger appears as one solid thing. But if we break it down and see its various aspects, we can see the ultimate nature of this experience. We can see that anger is impermanent, and it arises and passes away like a wave that comes and goes. We can see that anger is unsatisfactory; it does not bring us lasting joy. We can see that anger is empty of a "self" determining it; it does not arise according to our will, or whim, or wish. It arises when conditions are right for it to arise. We can see that it is not ours; we do not own it, we do not possess it. We cannot control anger's arising. We can only learn to relate to it in a skillful way.

If we look at the force of anger, we can, in fact, discover many positive aspects in it. Anger is not a passive, complacent state. It has incredible energy. Anger can impel us to let go of ways we may be inappropriately defined by the needs of others; it can teach us to say no. In this way it also serves our integrity, because anger can motivate us to turn from the demands of the outer world to the nascent voice of our inner world. It is a way to set boundaries and to challenge injustice at every level. Anger will not take things for granted or simply accept them mindlessly.

Anger also has the ability to cut through surface appearances; it does not just stay on a superficial level. It is very critical; it is very demanding. Anger has the power to pierce through the obvious to things that are more hidden. This is why anger may be transmuted to wisdom. By nature, anger has characteristics in common with wisdom.

Nevertheless, the unskillful aspects of anger are immense, and they far outweigh the positive aspects. The Buddha described it in this way: "Anger, with its poisoned source and fevered climax, murderously sweet, that you must slay to weep no more." It is sweet indeed! But the satisfaction we get from expressing anger is very short-lived, while the pain endures for a long time and debilitates us.

According to Buddhist psychology, the characteristic of anger is savageness. The function of anger is to burn up its own support, like a forest fire. It leaves us with nothing; it leaves us devastated. Just like a forest fire that ranges free and wild, anger can leave us in a place very far from where we intended to go. The deluding quality of anger is responsible for our losing ourselves in this way. When we are lost in anger, we do not see many options before us, and so we strike out recklessly.

Anger and aversion express themselves in acts of hostility and persecution. The mind becomes very narrow. It isolates someone or something, fixates on it, develops tunnel vision, sees no way out, fixes that experience, that person, or that object as being forever unchanging. Such aversion supports an endless cycle of harm and revenge.

We see this reality politically: with racial struggle, with class struggle, with national struggle, with religious hatreds. Anger can bind people to each other as strongly as desire, so that they drag each other along, connected through various kinds of revenge and counter-revenge, never being able to let go, never being able to be still. The playwright and statesman Vaclav Havel has noted insightfully that hatred has much in common with desire, that it is "the fixation on others, the dependence on them, and in fact the delegation of a piece of one's own identity to them. . . . The hater longs for the object of his hatred."

So it never ends, as long as people continue to relate in the same way. We see an oppressed people being hurt and then often taking power and behaving in exactly the same way toward some other people. Someone sends a letter accusing me, and I accuse them back.

How can we let go in such a situation? How can we change it? We can focus our attention more on the *suffering* of the situation, both our own and the suffering of others, rather than on our *anger*. We can ask ourselves whom we are really angry at. Mostly what we are angry at is the anger in the other person. It is almost as if the other person were an instrument for the anger that moves through them and motivates them to act in unskillful ways. We do not become angry at somebody's mouth when they are shouting at us; we are angry at the anger that is motivating them to shout. If we add anger to anger, we only serve to increase it.

In a well-known phrase, the Buddha said, "Hatred can never cease by hatred. Hatred can only cease by love. This is an eternal law." We can begin to transcend the cycle of aversion when we can stop seeing ourselves personally as agents of revenge. Ultimately, all beings are the owners of their own karma. If someone has caused harm, they will suffer. If we have caused harm, we will suffer. As the Buddha said in the *Dhammapada*:

> We are what we think.
> All that we are arises with our thoughts.
> With our thoughts we make the world.
> Speak or act with an impure mind

And trouble will follow you
As the wheel follows the ox that draws the cart. . . .
Speak or act with a pure mind
And happiness will follow you
As your shadow, unshakable.

Happiness and unhappiness depend upon our actions.

That does not mean that we sit back with glee, thinking, "You'll get yours in this life or the next." Rather, we understand that we do not have to be agents of revenge, that if people have caused suffering, they will suffer. This is an impersonal law, affecting us as well.

On the eve of his enlightenment, the Buddha, then known as the Bodhisattva, sat under the Bodhi Tree, determined not to move until he attained enlightenment. Mara, a mythic figure in the Buddhist cosmology, the "killer of virtue" and the "killer of life," recognizing that his kingdom of delusion was greatly jeopardized by the Bodhisattva's aspiration to awaken, came with many different challenges. Attempting to get the Bodhisattva to give up his resolve, he challenged him through lust, anger, and fear. He showered him with hailstorms, mud storms, and other travails. No matter what happened, the Bodhisattva sat serenely, unmoved and unswayed in his determination.

The final challenge of Mara was self-doubt. He said to the Bodhisattva, "By what right are you even sitting there with that goal? What makes you think you have the right even to aspire to full enlightenment, to complete awakening?" In response to that challenge, the Bodhisattva reached over and touched the earth. He called upon the earth itself to bear witness to all of the lifetimes in which he had practiced generosity, patience, and morality. Lifetime after lifetime he had built a wave of moral force that had given him the right to that aspiration.

When I think of the law of karma, I sometimes think of this story. The earth *is* bearing witness, and if we have caused suffering, we will suffer; if others have caused suffering they will suffer. Understanding this truth, we can let go. We can be free.

It so happened that on the very evening of the day I received that letter I reacted to so strongly, a friend brought a Tibetan lama to visit us at Insight Meditation Society. This lama had lived in a cave in the Himalayas for about fifteen years without ever leaving it. He was a master of the Tibetan practice of *tumo*, raising the body heat through the power of mind.

This lama had been approached in his cave and asked if he would consider going to America to be studied. He was told about how scientists, as they try to understand meditation, like to have effects that are measurable. Clearly, raising one's body heat through concentrating the mind is a very measurable thing. Because the Dalai Lama himself had made this request, the monk agreed to go. He came out of his cave and went straight to Boston. He was taken from the airport directly to the hospital, where he spent many days meditating while researchers kept taking his temperature.

At some point, our friend who had brought the lama there suggested that he take a break to come out to Insight Meditation Society, which is not too far from Boston. He came. When he walked through the door, the first thing he said was, "This place seems so different from the rest of America. What do you do here?" So we told him, and we ended up talking and spending the evening together.

This master of tumo had with him a young, articulate interpreter. The interpreter told us that this monk was considered quite extraordinary within the Tibetan tradition. He had become a monk quite late in life for that tradition, and he had gone very far in his meditation practice very fast, despite the fact that he had "skipped over" many aspects of spiritual training that the Tibetans consider necessary for such progress. He had not done the preliminary study or any of the preliminary meditation practices, which are considered to be absolutely essential in building a foundation before mastering more difficult and subtle practices. So the Tibetans considered him quite an anomalous puzzle.

We asked the lama, "Do you have any idea why you should have made such extraordinary progress in your practice, even though you did not fulfill these usual preliminaries?"

"Yes," he answered, "I do have an idea. When I was a layperson in Tibet, for many years I was a guerrilla fighter. Often I captured people and tortured and killed them. Then at some point in my life, I was captured myself by the Chinese and put in prison. I was tortured, and I underwent tremendous suffering. I made a commitment at that time not to hate the Chinese people."

The lama explained that he saw his situation in quite classical Buddhist terms. What he was experiencing at the hands of the Chinese, he understood to be the karmic fruit of his own previous actions. He pointed out that even if he had not seen it in those terms, he understood that nobody other than himself could *make* him suffer mentally. So he made a decision not to add the fires of hatred and bitterness to the terrible torment he was undergoing physically. He told us that he thought it was this decision that allowed him to make such extraordinary progress in his practice.

As this remarkable being was speaking, I was sitting there having images in my mind of the letter that I had been composing all day, saying, "That was your fault, and that was your fault, and *that* was your fault, too." I realized that I did not have to write it that way. Thanks to the propitious, timely example of the lama, I understood what is genuinely possible for human beings with a human heart. I understood, as the Buddha said, that "hatred will never cease by hatred." Never. "Hatred can only cease by love."

When our minds are full of anger and hatred toward others, in fact *we* are the ones who are actually suffering, caught in this mind state. But it is not so easy to access that place inside of us which can forgive, which can love. In some ways to be able to forgive, to let go, is a type of dying. It is the ability to say, "I am not that person anymore, and you are not that person anymore." Forgiveness allows us to recapture some part of ourselves that we left behind in bondage to a past event. Some part of our identity may also need to die in that letting go, so that we can reclaim the energy bound up in the past.

All of these teachings are available to us if we can be aware of what we are feeling in the deepest possible way, so that nothing is blocked from our consciousness. Then we can examine: What is our struggle? Why are we struggling? It is important to understand that no one thing makes us feel a certain way. Nothing stands alone in this conditioned world. We live in an interdependent reality, where we have the situation of the present moment and everything we are bringing to it as well.

Somebody could get up and do something in the middle of a room. Some people would become excited. Other people would be afraid. Some people would become angry. Other people would be amused. It is not that a given action, whatever it is, dictates a certain response. There is the situation, and there is everything we bring to it.

So we must take responsibility for our own mind. We live, hopefully, not just to drift along in the wake of different reactions, going up and down all of the time. Having a sense of purpose, such as the development of a loving heart, is the key to living a liberating practice.

If we can learn to see and understand all of these painful mind states of anger, fear, grief, disappointment, and guilt as states of aversion, we can learn to be free of them. Being free does not mean that aversion will never come up in our experience. Being free means that we can purify it. We can see it clearly, understand it, and learn not to be ruled by it. And having seen it clearly, which is the function of wisdom, we can also hold it in the vast, transforming field of acceptance.

EXERCISE

Forgiveness

In order to be released from deeply held aversion for ourselves and for others, we must be able to practice forgiveness. Forgiveness has the power to ripen forces of purity such as love, and affirms the qualities of patience and compassion. It creates the space for renewal, and a life free from bondage to the past.

When we are held prisoner by our own past actions, or the actions of others, our present life cannot be fully lived. The resentment, the partially experienced pain, the unwelcome inheritance we carry from the past, all function to close our hearts and thereby narrow our worlds.

The intention of forgiveness meditation is not to force anything, or to pretend to anything, or to forget about ourselves in utter deference to the needs of others. In fact, it is out of the greatest compassion for ourselves that we create the conditions for an unobstructed love, which can dissolve separation and relieve us of the twin burdens of lacerating guilt and perpetually unresolved outrage.

It is much more difficult to forgive than not to forgive. Political leaders seem to rely on this fact: it may be much easier to unite people with a bond of common hatred than with shared love. It is not so easy to access that place inside of us which can forgive, which can love. Remember, to be able to forgive is so deep a letting go that it is a type of dying. We must be able to say, "I am not that person anymore, and you are not that person anymore."

Forgiveness does not mean condoning a harmful action, or denying injustice or suffering. It should never be confused with being passive toward violation or abuse. Forgiveness is an inner relinquishment of guilt or resentment, both of which are devastating to us in the end. As forgiveness grows within us, it may take any outward form: we may seek to make amends, demand justice, resolve to be treated better, or simply leave a situation behind us.

The sense of psychological and spiritual well-being that comes from practicing forgiveness comes directly because this practice takes us to the edge of what we can accept. Being on the edge is challenging, wrenching, and transforming. The process of forgiveness demands courage and a continual remembering of where our deepest happiness lies. As Goethe said, "Our friends show us what we can do; our enemies show us what we must do."

It is indeed a process, which means that as you do the reflections, many conflicted emotions may arise: shame, anger, a sense of betrayal, confusion, or doubt. Try to allow such states to arise without judging them. Recognize them as natural occurrences, and then gently return your attention to the forgiveness reflection.

The reflection is done in three parts: asking forgiveness from those you have harmed, offering forgiveness to those who have harmed you, and offering forgiveness to yourself.

Sit comfortably, close your eyes, and let your breath be natural and uncontrolled. Begin with the recitation (silent or not, as you prefer): "If I have hurt or harmed anyone, knowingly or unknowingly, I ask their forgiveness." If different people, images, or scenarios come up, release the burden of guilt and ask for forgiveness: "I ask your forgiveness."

After some time, you can offer forgiveness to those who have harmed you. Don't worry if there is not a great rush of loving feeling; this is not meant to be an artificial exercise, but rather a way of honoring the powerful force of intention in our minds. We are paying respects to our ultimate ability to let go and begin again. We are asserting the human heart's capacity to change and grow and love. "If anyone has hurt or harmed me, knowingly or unknowingly, I forgive them." And, as different thoughts or images come to mind, continue the recitation, "I forgive you."

In the end, we turn our attention to forgiveness of ourselves. If there are ways you have harmed yourself, or not loved yourself, or not lived up to your own expectations, this is the time to let go of unkindness toward yourself because of what you have done. You can include any inability to forgive others that you may have discovered on your part in the reflection immediately preceding—that is not a reason to be unkind to yourself. "For all of the ways I have hurt or harmed myself, knowingly or unknowingly, I offer forgiveness."

Continue this practice as a part of your daily meditation, and allow the force of intention to work in its own way, in its own time.

EXERCISE
Seeing Goodness

Since the proximate cause, or most powerful conditioning force, for metta to arise is seeing the good in someone, we make an effort to turn our attention to any good we can find in a difficult person. We may be able to find one good quality even in someone with great character flaws, though we might feel reluctant to try.

The first time I was given the instruction to look for one good quality in a person I found difficult, I rebelled. I thought, "That's what superficial, gullible people do—they just look for the good in someone. I don't want to do that!" As I actually did the practice, however, I discovered that it had an important and powerful effect. In fact, it was doing just what it was supposed to do: looking for the good in someone did not cover up any of the genuine difficulties I found with that person, but allowed me to relate to them without my habituated defensiveness and withdrawal.

There was a person working at our center who was a source of conflict for almost everyone around. He was bombastic and cutting. One of the other people working there was diagnosed at that time with a progressive, painful, and potentially fatal disease. She had huge adjustments to make in terms of her self-image, aspirations, and level of functioning. One day I happened to witness an exchange between the two of them, where the difficult person was relating to my ill friend with compassion, humor, and grace. Whenever I thought about him afterward, I tried to remember that moment. In doing so, I noticed that the positive recollection did not function to deny my problems with his general behavior. Instead, it created a sense of warmth and spaciousness, a greater ease from which I could genuinely open to him.

There may be people who absolutely defy our ability (or willingness) to think of even one good thing about them. In that case, focus on the universal wish to be happy, which this difficult person also shares. All beings want to be happy, yet so very few know how. It is out of ignorance that any of us cause suffering, for ourselves or for others.

EXERCISE

The Difficult Person

As we come to sending metta to a person with whom we experience conflict, fear, or anger—known in the traditional texts as the enemy—we can reflect on this line from Rainer Maria Rilke: "Perhaps everything terrible is in its deepest being something that needs our love."

It is useful to begin with someone with whom the difficulty is relatively mild—not starting right away with an attempt to send metta to the one person who has hurt us the most in this lifetime. It is important to approach increasingly difficult people gradually. When I was first practicing metta in Burma, I received the instruction to send metta to a benefactor repeatedly, for about three weeks. The whole time I was secretly frustrated, thinking, "Why am I spending all this time sending metta to someone I already love? That's easy—I should be sending metta to my worst enemy. That's the only kind of love that really counts." Finally I expressed some of this to U Pandita, who laughed and said, "Why do you want to do things in the hardest way possible?" This practice is not meant to induce suffering, though it may reveal it. If a particular person has harmed us so grievously that it is very difficult to include them in the field of our loving care, then we approach sending them metta slowly, with a lot of care and compassion for ourselves.

Sending lovingkindness to a person with whom we have difficulty can be quite a challenge. We initiate the cultivation of metta by visualizing a benefactor, one toward whom it is most easy for us to feel love. In the same way that cultivating lovingkindness toward a benefactor is easy, feeling kindness toward an adversary can be just as difficult. In order to begin to develop metta toward a person with whom we have problems, we must first separate our vision of the person from the actions they commit that may upset or harm us. All beings are deserving of care, of well-being, of the gift of lovingkindness. In developing metta, we put aside the unpleasant traits of such a being and try instead to get in touch with the part of them that deserves to be loved.

Perhaps you can most easily feel metta for a difficult person if you imagine them as a vulnerable infant, or on their deathbed (but not with eager anticipation—be careful). You should allow yourself to be creative, daring, even humorous, in imagining situations where you can more readily feel kindness toward a difficult person. One student of mine chose as a difficult person someone who was loud, intrusive, and extremely talkative. She found she could only start sending this person metta if she imagined her sitting in a chair, bound and gagged. Another student was so afraid of his difficult person that he could only send him metta while imagining him well restrained in prison. As the strength of our metta grows, we can eventually reach a place where we sincerely extend wishes of well-being to the difficult people in our lives, even while we work to counter their actions and activities of which we disapprove.

Sit comfortably, and start with directing the metta phrases toward yourself, enveloping yourself with your own loving care. After some time, direct the phrases toward a benefactor, then a friend. If you have found a neutral person, you can then include them. You should turn your attention to the difficult person only after spending some time sending metta toward yourself and to those you find it relatively easy to feel metta for. Imagine the difficult person in any situation you wish. Get a sense of them by visualizing them or saying their name. If you can, contemplate one good thing about them. If you can't, remember that this person, just like ourselves, wishes to be happy, and makes mistakes out of ignorance. Direct the metta phrases toward them, whichever phrases you have been using. If saying, "May *you* be free from danger, may *you* be happy," brings up too much fear or sense of isolation for you, you can include yourself in the recitation: "May *we* be free from danger. May *we* be happy."

Gently continue to direct metta toward the difficult person, and accept the different feelings that may come and go. There may be sorrow, grief, anger—allow them to pass through you. If they become overwhelming, go back to sending metta to yourself or a good friend. You can also do some reflections to help hold those feelings in a different perspective. A classical one is to ask yourself, "Who is the one suffering from this anger? The person who has harmed me has gone on to live their life (or perhaps has died), while I am the one sitting here feeling the persecution, burning, and constriction of anger. Out of compassion for myself, to ease my own heart, may I let go."

Another reflection is done by turning your mind to the suffering of the difficult person, rather than viewing their actions only as bad or wrong. Compassion is the refinement of love that opens to suffering. When we feel anger, fear, or jealousy, if we feel open to the pain of these states rather than disgraced by their arising, then we will have compassion for ourselves. When we see others lost in states of anger, fear, and so on, and we remember how painful those states are, we can have compassion for those people as well.

When you can, return to directing the metta phrases toward the difficult person. You can go back and forth between yourself, a friend, the reflections, and the difficult person.

You may find yourself expressing greater lovingkindness in actual life situations before you experience a greater depth of loving feeling in your formal meditation practice. Sometimes in difficult encounters there is more patience than before, more willingness to listen than before, and more clarity than before. I had a student who did an intensive metta retreat and chose a former partner in his firm as his difficult person. Negotiations for the partner's departure from the firm were still going on and were highly acrimonious. My student dutifully spent his time sending metta to his former partner, but felt mostly either boredom or irritation. He was astonished upon returning to work, and the next negotiation session, to find himself greeting his former partner with some warmth. The partner was astonished as well. He looked at my friend for some time and then said, "Is that *you*?"

Be patient with yourself in this practice, and try not to hold rigid expectations of what you should be experiencing. Strong expectations detract from our capacity for joy and will often lead to more anger. When we have rigid expectations, we can feel a great sense of helplessness if those expectations are not quickly met. We see our actions as being fruitless, not going anywhere, and we get lost in contempt or self-condemnation. Remember that whatever anger, fear, or sorrow arises will pass away, and we can always return to the intention to care for ourselves and for all beings. Beginning again and again is the actual practice, not a problem to be overcome so that one day we can come to the "real" meditation.

EXERCISE

Difficult Aspects of Oneself

As an alternative to choosing a difficult person, you can experiment with directing metta toward a difficult aspect of yourself. There may be physical or emotional aspects of yourself you have struggled with, denied, avoided, been at war with. Sit quietly, sending yourself metta. After some time, turn your attention to the loneliness, anger, disability, addiction, or whatever aspect of your mind or body you feel most estranged from. Healing begins with the open, compassionate acknowledgment of these unpleasant aspects of our lives. Surround the painful element of your experience with the warmth and acceptance of metta. You can use phrases such as, "May I accept this," "May I be filled with lovingkindness toward this," "May I use the pain of this experience for the welfare of all." Feel free to use whatever phrases come to your mind, and return periodically to directing metta to yourself with your customary phrases.

6

Breaking Open the Loving Heart

The thought manifests as the word;
The word manifests as the deed;
The deed develops into habit;
And habit hardens into character.
So watch the thought and its ways with care,
And let it spring from love
Born out of concern for all beings.

—*The Buddha*

It is only due to our concepts that we feel separate from the world. We are isolated by ideas of inadequacy, ideas of danger, ideas of loneliness, and ideas of rejection. While we may indeed face external difficulties, our thoughts can amplify them—or even create them, leading us deeper into delusion. If we do not want to be enslaved by our thoughts, we can choose to transform our minds. In any given moment, do I choose to strengthen the delusion of separation or the truth of connection?

One fall I was teaching at the Insight Meditation Society, which is located in a rural area. Each morning I would go for a walk very early, just as it was getting light. This walk took me past the mobile home where Max lived. Max was a huge dog—he looked like a cross between a Doberman pinscher and a mountain lion. I started hearing reports that Max had grown agitated and aggressive, snarling at people and threatening to attack them. I had been experiencing a series of unfortunate events that fall, and I thought I might end this cycle of difficulty by being torn limb from limb by this dog.

Every day at dawn I would set out with a certain "Max consciousness," my fear growing with each step as I approached his territory. For many days Max had not been in the yard as I passed, but I was becoming increasingly tense about the prospect of an encounter. As the days went on, I found that my very first thought when I awoke in the morning centered on Max and my fear of him. I had read that His Holiness the Dalai Lama's very first thought upon waking is a prayer of love and compassion, dedicating all of the coming actions of the day to the benefit of all living beings. Starting the day as I was, in fear of Max, was beginning to seem pretty ignoble.

Finally, one morning Max was there. From far away I saw him sitting in the twilight. Fear rose sharply. I proceeded slowly, with each step seeing him as increasingly separate from myself and as a tremendous threat: "He's out there, he's very big, and he's getting closer." Finally I arrived. Max stood up. I stopped. We looked at each other. And then I blurted out the first thing that came to mind: "Max, Maxine is my middle name. People used to call me Max, too, you know!" We looked at each other for a few moments more, then Max sat down again, and I walked on.

From that point on I saw that love was a choice for me in many different situations. I developed a relationship to Max, a feeling of connection. He seemed like someone I knew, someone who might be in a bad state, who might even lose control and actually try to hurt me, but someone who was nevertheless a friend. I did not at all stop being careful. But Max ceased to be a terrible, alien creature, a great, hulking beast out there waiting to get me. He stopped being the "other."

Fear is the primary mechanism sustaining the concept of the "other," and reinforcing the subsequent loneliness and distance in our lives. Ranging from numbness to terror, fear constricts our hearts and binds us to false and misleading ways of viewing life. The fallacy of separate existence cloaks itself in the beguiling forms of our identifications: "This is who I am," or "This is all I can ever be." We identify with a fragment of reality rather than with the whole.

A modern astronomical view says that everything in the universe is moving uniformly away from everything else in all directions into space, so that there is no center point in the cosmos at all. We live with no fixed reference point. From one perspective, this understanding produces the desolate feeling that there is no home. But from another perspective, this realization shows us directly that every point is home. We are free; we do not need to fix on a single center for refuge, for safety. This is love, this is happiness, where our refuge is unbounded, and we are always at home. As the Buddha said, "They abide in peace who do not abide anywhere."

When we identify with the body as a separate self, as our only home, we think we must control it in order to preserve our sense of who we are. But we cannot control sickness or old age or death. If we try, we bear the inevitable burdens of hopelessness and powerlessness. When we conceive of ourselves as finite and separate, how fearful death becomes! What would we fear if we experienced ourselves to be part of the whole of nature, moving and changing, being born and dying?

We would then see that our bodies are joined with the planet in a continual, rhythmic exchange as matter and energy flow back and forth between ourselves and the environment. This is breathing. With each breath we exchange carbon dioxide from within us for oxygen outside us. Normally we take this process for granted, but this exchange, this connection that is going on every moment, is actually the experience of being alive. We do not live as isolated fragments, completely separate, but as parts of a great, dynamic, mutable whole.

Another prevalent concept we suffer under is identification with the mind as a separate, permanent entity, as our true abiding. With this conceptual framework, we can easily say to someone or to ourselves, "Well, you are this way and you'll always be this way." Once I was teaching with Joseph Goldstein when someone came to see him in great distress. The man said, "I just had a terrible experience!" Joseph quite naturally said, "Well, tell me what happened." The man said, "I was meditating, and I felt this tension in my jaw, and realized what an uptight person I am, how I have never been able to get close to anyone, and how I will be alone for the rest of my life." Trying to help him break free of his conceptual overlay and return to an awareness of his actual experience, Joseph pointed out, "You mean you felt some tension in your jaw." The man was plagued by his projections. "Yes, I see what an incredibly uptight person I am, how I always have been and I always will be, how it will never ever change and I will never get close to anyone for the entire rest of my life." As you might imagine, Joseph kept repeating, "You mean you felt some tension in your jaw." To my bemusement they continued on for some time in this vein, until finally Joseph said, "You are having a painful experience. Why are you adding an immutable, horrible self-image to it?"

Concepts can rule us in many different ways. When we are caught in the concepts of separation, we suffer distance and alienation. We need to defend ourselves at all times because the world seems very threatening. When we experience a strong idea of separate, immutable self and other, it seems as though there is constantly a great big "other" out there. To bear this danger, we need to hold ourselves in tense readiness, waiting for every impact. Once, a woman attending a nonresidential metta weekend in New York City was on her way back to the retreat site on Saturday morning when a man approached her on the railway platform and asked a question about the train schedule. Even though she was holding a schedule in her hand, her thought was, "He looks really weird! I'd better get rid of him." Her initial claim to have no knowledge of the trains was belied by her clearly visible schedule. She tried a few ploys to have him go away, to no avail. Finally, she randomly pointed to someone else on the platform and said, "You should go ask him." The stranger looked at her uneasily and said, "Oh no! I couldn't ask him—he looks really weird!"

Of course there are times when we face actual danger, and enmity, and desperation. To have metta in these circumstances does not mean we are passive, or mindless to our needs in the situation. Just as I did with Max, we have to know how to take care of ourselves and act appropriately when facing different conditions. And, just as I learned to do with Max, we can learn to do that without the constant fear or aching loneliness that the sense of immutable "other" leaves us with.

The legacy of separation impoverishes the spirit. Seeking only to protect ourselves, we cannot genuinely connect with others, we cannot see what needs our love, and we struggle with terrible aloneness. In trying to reach others from the stance of our isolation, we are like weary travelers preparing for a dangerous border crossing, cautiously hoping to reach a new land and make contact, secretly believing it will not be possible. Veering between fitful hope and underlying insecurity, we have no peace. Imagine the relief of discovering that there is no such border to be crossed! It is only through seeing our fundamental connection with the world that a life of true peace becomes possible.

The ways in which we direct our minds to cultivate this seeing are all-important. This transformation of mind, releasing the burden of concepts, is not just theoretical. There is a path to actualize it. Again and again in his teachings, the Buddha explores love and connectedness. Through meditation and the brahmaviharas he offers us the possibility to radically change our relationship to life.

When we learn to move beyond mistaken concepts and see clearly, we no longer solidify reality. We see waves coming and going, arising and passing. We see that life, composed of this mind and body, is in a state of continual, constant transformation and flux. There is always the possibility of radical change. Every moment—not just poetically or figuratively, but literally—every moment we are dying and being reborn, we and all of life.

Without the rigidity of concepts, the world becomes transparent and illuminated, as though lit from within. With this understanding, the interconnectedness of all that lives becomes very clear. We see that nothing is stagnant and nothing is fully separate, that who we are, what we are, is intimately woven into the nature of life itself. Out of this sense of connection, love and compassion arise.

This is a beautiful expression of our unity, by Susan Griffin in *Woman and Nature:*

We say that you cannot divert the river from the riverbed. We say that everything is moving, and we are part of this motion, that the soil is moving, that the water is moving. We say that the earth draws water to her from the clouds. We say the rainfall parts on each side of the mountain like the parting of our hair, and that the shape of the mountain tells where the water has passed. We say this water washes the soil from the hillsides, that the rivers carry sediment; that rain, when it splashes, carries small particles. That the soil itself flows with water and streams underground. We say that water is taken up into the roots of plants, into stems. That it washes down hills into rivers, that these rivers flow to the sea, that from the sea and the sunlight, this water rises to the sky. This water is carried into clouds and comes back as rain, comes back as fog, comes back as dew, as wetness in the air. We say everything comes back. You cannot divert the river from the riverbed. We say every act has its consequences. That this place has been shaped by the river, and the shape of this place tells the river where to go. We say look how the water flows from this place and returns as rainfall. Everything returns, we say, and one thing follows another. There are limits, we say, on what can be done, and everything moves. We are all a part of this motion, we say, and the way of the river is sacred, and this grove of trees is sacred, and we ourselves, we tell you, are sacred.

Love and concern for all are not things some of us are born with and others are not. Rather, they are results of what we do with our minds: We can choose to transform our minds so that they embody love, or we can allow them to develop habits and false concepts of separation.

The Buddha said, "So watch the thought and its ways with care, and let it spring from love born out of concern for all beings." We are not urged to *make* thought spring from love born out of concern for all beings. Rather, we are advised to *let* it spring from the love that is our true nature.

If we cannot heal the rupture between ourselves and the rest of life, created by mistaken concepts, we remain lost, uncertain about what our lives mean and where we belong. Chased by concepts of separate self and distant other, as though pursued by furious enemies, we run until we are lost, hiding in whatever places seem to offer us safety. Our safest haven, however, may be found neither in running nor in hiding, but in staying still. The Taoist philosopher Chuang Tzu told this story:

> There was a man so displeased by the sight of his own shadow and so displeased with his own footsteps that he determined to get rid of both. The method he hit upon was to run away from them. So he got up and ran. But every time he put his foot down there was another step, while his shadow kept up with them without the slightest difficulty. He attributed his failure to the fact that he was not running fast enough. So he ran faster and faster, without stopping, until he finally dropped dead. He failed to realize that if he merely stepped into the shade, his shadow would vanish, and if he sat down and stayed still, there would be no more footsteps.

When we make the courageous choice to be still, rather than running away, we have the chance to establish a relationship with what *is*. When I actually stopped and looked at Max, I found something of myself.

Being still in meditation reveals the truth of our lives. The fact is, we never have been separate; we have never been alone or apart, neither Max and I, nor any other being and myself. Even my worst enemy and myself are not wholly separate.

Relieved of this mistaken duality, we witness the falling away of the feelings that flow from ignorance. Feelings of isolation and fear, feelings of fragmentation and alienation drop away, because there is nothing any longer to sustain them, to nourish them.

My colleague Sylvia Boorstein was once on a plane that developed a problem with the hydraulic system. The passengers were told that the plane was turning back to the airport, which would take about forty minutes. They were instructed in the position to take in an emergency landing and were told that their shoes would be collected by the flight attendants, and that they should remove pens from their pockets and their eyeglasses as well. This was obviously serious! Every once in a while the announcement would be issued: "We will be landing in thirty minutes . . . in twenty minutes . . ." Soon after the very first announcement of trouble, Sylvia began doing metta meditation. She began with the thirteen people in her immediate family—her husband, her children and their spouses, and her grandchildren. "May Collin be happy, may Nathan be happy, may Grace be happy. . . ." She continued on with this group of beloved ones as the plane got closer and closer to the airport. "We will be landing in fifteen minutes . . . in ten minutes . . ." At one point Sylvia thought, "Well, in a few minutes either I will be alive or I will be dead." In seeking to reach beyond her immediate circle, in circumstances that had to include the possibility of imminent death, Sylvia found that the next logical group she was inspired to send metta to was all beings everywhere, without distinction, without exclusion, without exception. It made no sense to separate, to close off to anyone in what might prove to be the end of her life.

As we open, we uncover the mind's inherent ability to heal, to grow, to change. Being still, we see the power of the mind, which is the strength of our own capacity to love and connect. Actual love is the true seeing of our oneness, our nonseparateness. As we discover this capacity to love, we develop intimacy with ourselves and others. We develop the strength and compassion to live with integrity and, one day, to die with peace.

Our freedom to love arises from discovering that we can live without the concept of self and other. The joy of this discovery is incomparably greater than what many of us have previously known, or even imagined—so much so that our entire view of life changes.

Being free from concepts is like going backstage in a theater and suddenly realizing how much of our engagement with the drama has come from mere appearances: the costumes, the makeup, the staging, the lighting, and actors projecting artificial personae. It is liberating to realize that we are, in effect, "making it all up." We are playing on the stage set, lost in the costumes and the lighting. We are creating boundaries and divisions according to our histories, our fears, our needs, and our habits. But what is the substance of these boundaries? Where can they be found, in truth?

I have been to Russia several times, beginning in 1988, to teach meditation there. Being there is especially poignant for me, since that is where my family originally came from. Many of the people I spend time with there look very familiar, as if they could be my cousins. The last time I went, economic conditions were terribly difficult.

One Russian friend said to me, "I don't know what I'll do when my shoes wear out, since I can't afford to buy new ones." As he described his situation, I felt the shame, the fear, and the pain he was expressing as if it were my own, as though it were happening inside my own family.

Only later did I think of how many other people in the world cannot afford new shoes, people I do not feel at all connected to because I do not meet them in the ordinary course of events. How many children in the world have never even had a pair of shoes, let alone a new pair? Does someone have to resemble my cousins to be included in my sense of family?

We mark off the territory of our identifications, both personal and group, as though they had intrinsic meaning, whereas it is only like drawing lines in space. On an earlier trip to the Soviet Union, just as constraints on freedom of speech were being lifted, I was shocked to stand on street corners and hear representatives of the far right state authoritatively that only Jews and blacks could contract AIDS, and that it was a conspiracy of the West to delude the Russian people to think otherwise. Now, in the Soviet Union of that time, dentists were often not sterilizing drills because it wore out the parts and they could not get replacements. Orthopedic surgeons were encouraging patients to try to get their own razor blades on the black market for the surgical incision, since the scalpels were so worn out and were no longer being sterilized. I stood on some of those street corners and wondered how much suffering and death might come about because of the ignorance and identification being purveyed there.

The concept of self and other also manifests as persecution, war, and oppression. At one point during the Vietnam War, General William Westmoreland, the commander of U.S. forces in Vietnam, made a comment that revealed his belief that Asians are not like us; this allowed him to wage war on them. They do not mind dying, the general said, explaining that Asians do not have the same respect for life that we do. We often feel alienated from people of other races and cultures who do not look like us, and even from people who do look like us. Like pioneers who circled the wagons around their encampments to protect themselves, we divide the world into "us" and "them." But as life goes on and such boundaries become relics of the past, we do not know, finally, whether we belong inside or outside the arbitrary circle.

We can even experience "otherness" from ourselves. We can experience our internal disconnection as a great, hulking, terrible beast inside us, like Max, crouched and ready to attack. As Ajahn Sumedho, an American Buddhist monk and meditation teacher, has said, "It's as though we fear there is some kind of monster hiding inside us, waiting to come up and drive us permanently insane."

Indeed, there is a Max within. In fact, there is more than one; there are a lot of Maxes in our own minds. There is anger, lust, jealousy, and greed—the list can go on and on. Can we recognize these forces and see them as friends who might be in a terrible state and thus need our compassion and care? Can we truly love ourselves, all aspects of ourselves? Can we give this force of love not only to ourselves, but also to others?

Perhaps the most vital transformation we undergo when we practice meditation and the brahma-viharas is the transformation in our perception of what is possible. Now we are no longer bound by previous ideas of limitation: "I'd better not love anymore, because I have reached my limit." I have sat in wonder at times in my meditation practice, thinking, "Can I actually be feeling this much love?"

The meditation practices of lovingkindness, compassion, sympathetic joy, and equanimity help us to find union within ourselves and with the world outside. Eventually we see that literally there is no inside and outside. The one is just one.

Our potential as human beings is measureless; it is vast, unfathomable. Our minds are incredibly dynamic, powerful, energetic force fields. Recognizing these realities is the ground for seeing that what we care about and what we do with our minds makes a difference. When we practice the brahma-viharas, we can benefit ourselves and all of life. Our lives are our own artistic medium, and there is nothing holding us back from shaping them except our limited ideas of what is possible.

To speak of the power of mind is not to deny in any way the pain caused by external, material conditions. It is a terrible thing to live in war and poverty, to face being killed, not to have enough to feed yourself or your children, not to have medicine that could cure your illness or the disease of a loved one. But, at the same time, it is crucial to maintain a vision of life that includes the tremendous effect of our minds on our reality.

I have met beggars on the streets of India whose spirits were enormous. I have seen a beggar in Calcutta, with no arms or legs, because of leprosy, crawling along the streets with a bucket in her mouth into which people dropped money. Despite her suffering, she wanted to live. I have also known people here in the United States who have had healthy bodies and financial resources, who have received care from others who love them, and yet these people have wanted to die. They have been terribly depressed and have wanted to kill themselves.

Some people, like the beggar in Calcutta, are faced with personal limitations, while others encounter limitations because people have actually tried to harm or destroy them. One of the most moving experiences I have ever had was at a conference where, during one panel presentation, almost all of the panelists described tremendous suffering in their lives. There were terrible stories: a woman who had spent her childhood in a Nazi concentration camp, a Vietnamese woman who at different times had been captured and tortured by each side in the Vietnam War. Everybody on that panel expressed a heartfelt commitment to create a world where no one would have to experience what they themselves had experienced. For each of them the root of that commitment was recognizing that such atrocities transpire because of people's constructing a sense of "us" and "them." Remarkably, their dedication to deconstructing the sense of "us" and "them" included the people who had harmed them.

Recognizing the power of our minds means that even as unfortunate or terrible things happen to us, we can receive them in a more spacious and ultimately more enlightened way. The Buddha taught his students to develop a power of love so strong that the mind becomes like space that cannot be tainted. If someone throws paint, it is not the air that will change color. Space will not hold the paint; it will not grasp it in any way. Only the walls, the barriers to space, can be affected by the paint.

The Buddha taught his students to develop a power of love so strong that their minds become like a pure, flowing river that cannot be burned. No matter what kind of material is thrown into it, it will not burn. Many experiences—good, bad, and indifferent—are thrown into the flowing river of our lives, but we are not burned, owing to the power of the love in our hearts.

The concepts of separateness that have dominated our lives have produced tremendous suffering. What we have taken to be real is in fact a hallucination. The division between self and other is the degradation of our highest human potential: the liberation of the mind that is love. The critical moment of the path, which breaks open the loving heart, is the realization that we have never existed as separate, isolated beings. When wisdom recognizes our oneness and sees the interconnectedness of all beings, it fills us with a degree of happiness that transforms our lives.

This is the Buddha's offering of a path for the fruition of understanding: fearlessness, connectedness, and love, which we can develop through practice of the brahma-viharas. The path cultivates openness that is empowered by the truth of non-separateness, so that it can only bring happiness. Fueled by this happiness, we rest in the naturalness of a loving heart. The sense of separation is uprooted precisely because it no longer finds a place to take root. Just as paint does not affect space, the power of love is so strong it cannot be tainted by anything in this evanescent world.

EXERCISE

Lovingkindness for All Beings

We dissolve the concepts of separateness that have ruled our lives by practicing metta for all beings without exception.

Lovingkindness for all beings is the foundation of moral and spiritual awakening. As Krishnamurti said, "There is no silence without love." Those looking for silence, for the end of the conditioning of self and other, for profound transformation, need to look at the power of developing love for all.

Begin by sitting and extending the feeling of metta, which is friendship, caring, and kindness, to yourself. Then, as a transition, you can reflect on the fact that all beings want to be happy: "Just as I want to be happy, all beings want to be happy." Then begin to direct metta to all beings, including yourself.

Traditionally this is first done by formulating different categories that convey to you a sense of the boundlessness of life, the immeasurable nature of sentient existence. Examples are "all beings," "all living beings," "all creatures," "all individuals," and "all those in existence." Using a few different categories that point to this vastness, combine them with your regular metta phrases: "May all beings be free from danger. May they [or "we," if you prefer] have mental happiness. May they have physical happiness. May they have ease of well-being."

"May all living beings be free from danger. May they have mental happiness. May they have physical happiness. May they have ease of well-being."

"May all creatures be free from danger. May they have mental happiness. May they have physical happiness. May they have ease of well-being."

"May all individuals be free from danger. May they have mental happiness. May they have physical happiness. May they have ease of well-being."

"May all those in existence be free from danger. May they have mental happiness. May they have physical happiness. May they have ease of well-being."

Repeat the metta phrases you have chosen, and extend them to all beings everywhere, without division, without exclusion, and without end.

EXERCISE

Lovingkindness toward Groups

The Buddha talked about doing metta in such a way that we begin to care for beings as a mother would protect her only child. To even approach this capacity, over time we must see where our barriers have been erected and our resistances have been fed. One way to use metta to see our concepts of division, to melt the barriers we have maintained, and to move toward unification with all beings is to send metta to different groups of beings.

In doing this we try to include pairs of opposite or complementary sets of groups, so as to ultimately include all beings everywhere. An example is "all females" and then "all males." Females and males as categories encompass not just human beings but all femininity and all masculinity. You may find an easy affinity with one gender grouping, and dis-ease or resistance when sending metta to the other gender group, but the very discovery of that fact is an important part of this exploration.

Other examples of groupings include "all enlightened beings" and "all those in ignorance" (the groups don't need to be equal in size, just complementary); "all those known to me" and "all those unknown to me"; "those near" and "those far"; "those being born," "those in existence," and "those dying."

Classically, there are seven groups used: all females, all males, all enlightened ones, all unenlightened ones, all devas and *brahmas* (supremely happy beings), all humans (those who experience a mixture of pleasure and pain), and all those in the lower worlds (those who experience great suffering).

For each sitting, you can use the classical list of seven or create a list of your own groups. As you become more comfortable with this practice, the groupings should include personal challenges, like "all those who are suffering" and "all those who are causing suffering." See where you would prefer to exclude beings from your metta, and slowly dissolve that boundary.

EXERCISE

Walking Meditation

A meditation that can be both insightful and enjoyable involves sending metta while walking outside. Walk at a normal pace, and begin by directing the metta phrases to yourself. As different beings come by, offer them metta: "May you be free from danger . . ." You don't know who will come into your field of awareness: friends, neutral beings, those who bring up fear or aversion within us. Alternate between sending lovingkindness to yourself and to those coming by. The very fact that who comes by is outside of your control makes it an adventure in metta. Remember that "beings" includes nonhuman beings as well, so depending on where you are, you might find them flying by, crawling by, hopping by, or slithering by, as well as using the modes of locomotion we associate with humans.

In time you can use this meditation anywhere. Sitting or walking, in any situation where you meet many beings—at the supermarket, on a bus or an airplane, in a waiting room. This exercise helps develop a greater vibrancy and strength of metta, as well as suppleness of mind. It reminds us that metta can be a valid option for us in an ever-widening set of circumstances, until it reaches true vastness.

EXERCISE

The Ten Directions

Another form of boundless metta meditation is to send lovingkindness to beings in the ten directions: east, southeast, south, southwest, west, northwest, north, northeast, above, and below. You can start with any direction you wish, and either guide the force of metta in that direction with a felt sense or include the direction verbally in the phrase, or both.

As you sit, you can use whatever categories you have become familiar with to express the limitless forms of life, such as "all beings," "all living beings," "all creatures," "all individuals," "all those in existence." You can also use the different groupings you have been using, such as "all females" and "all males." You can use the groupings alone or in combination with the different representations of limitless life.

Now, as you send metta, include the direction as well: "May all beings to the east be happy." "May all living beings to the east be happy." "May all creatures to the east be happy." . . . "May all females to the east be happy." "May all males to the east be happy."

Metta sent to beings in the ten directions, with its qualities of nonexclusivity and boundless extension, helps us recognize our union with all of life. Limitless friendship links us with the clear awareness of interconnectedness. As we continue to practice in this way, the power of love in our minds begins to resemble the vast openness of space, which cannot be tainted or marred.

7

Developing the Compassionate Heart

I teach one thing and one only: that is, suffering and the end of suffering.

—The Buddha

MANY YEARS AGO, when I was living in India and practicing meditation in Bodh Gaya, I had gone with a friend to spend a few days in Calcutta. When it was time to leave, we found we were running late to catch our train back. The only way we could get to the train station on time was to take a rickshaw. In many other places in India, rickshaws are pulled by people on bicycles or motorbikes, but in Calcutta they are actually pulled by people running on foot. So, even though we hated the thought of being carried by another human being in this way, we caught a rickshaw to the station.

The rickshaw man took us by shortcuts, through dark streets and down back alleys. At one point, suddenly out of nowhere, an extremely big man approached the rickshaw driver and stopped him. Then he looked at me, grabbed me, and tried to pull me off the rickshaw. I looked around the streets for help. There were a lot of people everywhere, as there often are in India, but I did not see a single friendly face.

I thought, "Oh my God, this guy is going to drag me off and rape me. Then he's going to kill me, and nobody is going to help me!" My friend who was sitting with me in the rickshaw managed to push the drunken man away and urged the rickshaw driver to go on. So we escaped and got to the station.

I was very shaken and upset when we arrived in Bodh Gaya. I told Munindra, one of my meditation teachers, what had happened.

He looked at me and said, "Oh, Sharon, with all the lovingkindness in your heart, you should have taken your umbrella and hit that man over the head with it!"

Sometimes we think that to develop an open heart, to be truly loving and compassionate, means that we need to be passive, to allow others to abuse us, to smile and let anyone do what they want with us. Yet this is not what is meant by compassion. Quite the contrary. Compassion is not at all weak. It is the strength that arises out of seeing the true nature of suffering in the world. Compassion allows us to bear witness to that suffering, whether it is in ourselves or others, without fear; it allows us to name injustice without hesitation, and to act strongly, with all the skill at our disposal. To develop this mind state of compassion, the second of the brahma-viharas, is to learn to live, as the Buddha put it, with sympathy for all living beings, without exception.

The feeling we call compassion is often misunderstood, however. The first time I was teaching meditation in the Soviet Union, I talked a lot about compassion. As the words were being translated into Russian, I kept getting the funny feeling that I was not conveying my meaning clearly. I finally asked the interpreter, "When I say 'compassion,' what do you say?" He answered, "Oh, I describe a state of being terribly overcome by somebody's sorrow, like having a stake through your heart and having the burden of somebody's pain burdening you as well." I just sat there thinking, "Oh, no."

It is easy to understand how the meaning of compassion could be taken to include this state of being overcome by the suffering of another.

When it is translated literally from the Pali and Sanskrit word *karuna*, "compassion" means experiencing a trembling or quivering of the heart in response to a being's pain. But compassion is not debilitating, as suggested by the state described by the interpreter. To be overwhelmed by pain can lead us into despair, grief, aimlessness, even anger. This is not compassion. Ram Dass and Paul Gorman, in their book *How Can I Help?* write: ". . . it's one thing to have one's heart engaged, and another to have it overwhelmed or broken. Here lies our aversion to suffering." If we feel that our hearts will break, that we will be overwhelmed, that we cannot bear what is going on, we find it difficult to open to pain—yet that is the basis of compassion.

The first step in developing true compassion is being able to recognize, to open to, and to acknowledge that pain and sorrow exist. Everywhere, absolutely everywhere, in one way or another, beings are suffering. Some suffering is intense and terrible; some is quiet and small.

W. H. Auden wrote:

> About suffering they were never wrong,
> The Old Masters: how well they understood
> Its human position; How it takes place
> While someone else is eating or opening a window or just
>   walking dully along. . . .

While suffering is not all there is in life, it is a thread that needs to be recognized clearly if we are to develop true compassion.

If we look at our own experience, it comes as no big surprise that suffering exists. We have our ups and downs, we have pain or loss or sorrow, times when we do not get what we want, or we do get what we want but it goes away or proves to be not what we wanted after all. We all experience this pattern. Because we know this experience as real, not receiving external confirmation of our perception is actually far more painful than a frank acknowledgment would be.

Yet we are brought up with the feeling that suffering is somehow wrong or to be avoided. We get the idea that suffering is unbearable and should not even be faced. So we create a society that accommodates our need to deny pain as best we can. We use material consumption and painkillers to avoid suffering. We take people who are different, people who are in trouble, people who are old, people who are dying, and put them out of sight in institutions. These are forms of suffering we all share, but there is so much humiliation and bitterness about getting sick or growing old or dying that we feel we have to hide our pain. One striking example of this pervasive denial occurred when Ronald Reagan was first running for president. The media were filled with images of the American family, which at that time was almost a sacred entity. According to the social myth being propagated, there were many issues the courts would no longer have to decide or the legislatures consider, because "the American family" was going to take care of them. This was a picture of the American family without suffering or conflict. All of its members were communicating and taking good care of one another. There was so much familial respect and closeness that no intervention on the part of government agencies would be necessary.

When I read these descriptions in the newspaper or heard them on the radio or television, I would think, "What families are they talking about?" They were not talking about any that I had ever met or heard of. They were not talking about the families with violence and alcoholism, or even the ones where people hadn't really talked to each other for many years.

I do not mean to imply that there is no happiness in family life. There can be great happiness in family life, but how often is it so very perfect as this political vision implied? No wonder people feel terrible about their own situations! Look at what is being held up as real.

Thus we live like children growing up in a dysfunctional family, where there is conflict but no one ever speaks about it. The pain is denied, as if the children could be spared the awful truth. But they always know what is going on, though they are never given any validation for this understanding and its attendant feelings. This is how people learn not to trust their own experience. Through denial, a tremendous disparity is created between inner reality and the circumstances of the external world.

A story from the great Hindu epic, the *Mahabharata*, illustrates this human drive to deny. Yudhistara is asked, "What is the most wondrous thing in the entire world?" He replies, "The most wondrous thing in the entire world is that all around us people can be dying and we don't believe it can happen to us." It is as though we live our lives with a big surprise waiting at the end. Many times when I have stood in line at the checkout counter of the supermarket, I have seen the tabloid headlines telling about Elvis Presley, who is still alive and has been sighted somewhere. "ELVIS SPOTTED IN FLORIDA!" or California, or even once on Mars. Why can't he have died? People do die. Why is that so impossible to accept?

When we deny our experience, we are always moving away from something real to something fabricated. To live by this web of legend will always harm us. The truth may be difficult to open to, but it will never hurt us. What a tremendous relief to have the actual truth openly spoken: "There is suffering in this world." Everything is up-front. There are no games, no pretense, no denial. To acknowledge the truth of suffering allows us to feel our unity with others. The goal of our spiritual practice is to be able to understand, to be able to look without illusion at what is natural in this life, at what is actually happening for others and for ourselves. This willingness to see what is true is the first step in developing compassion.

More difficult than *acknowledging* pain, however, is *opening* to it. This is the second step in developing compassion: opening to pain and establishing an appropriate relationship to it. In order to genuinely open to pain, we may have to do so a little bit at a time. If our opening is forced or contrived, our sense of purpose may shatter.

Sometimes, when we begin to open to suffering, we displace it, so that even though we see it, we also have the sense of being able to control it, as if we could turn it off and on. This tendency to displace may be why people can so avidly read about violence in newspapers or magazines or watch it constantly in movies or on TV. We look at tragedy with the hope that we can control it by turning the dial.

When we do not feel in control, very often we feel righteous anger, fear, or grief. In Buddhist psychology these are known as compassion's near enemies, because they may disguise themselves as compassion. Compassion's *far* enemy, cruelty, is so clearly the opposite state that it is easy to detect. It can be harder to distinguish when we are lost in aversion. We may feel angry at injustice or outraged to see or hear of misuses of power, whether in families, communities, or political systems. We may become afraid ourselves when we witness the fear of others. We may feel sorrow and grief over the losses suffered by others. All of these feelings are similar to compassion, "the trembling of the heart." But compassion is quite different, in fact, from anger, fear, and grief. These states of aversion can drain us, perhaps destroy us. This is not to say that it is wrong to feel them, but we must be able to look at our experience truthfully and see the consequences of one set of responses as opposed to another.

Once I gave a talk on the differences between aversion and compassion. Someone came to speak to me, quite upset. He told me about his sister who was severely brain-damaged and in a nursing home, all too often receiving substandard care. He insisted that only his repeated, infuriated interventions were keeping her alive in that institution. His whole body was trembling as he spoke. After some moments, I asked him, "What is your inner reality like?" He replied, "I'm dying inside. The anger is killing me!" Certainly there are injustices to be named in this world, and hate-filled situations to be changed, and inequities to be remedied. There is appropriate treatment to be demanded, without prejudice or fear. But can we do these things without destroying ourselves through anger?

The state of compassion as the trembling of the heart arises with a quality of equanimity. Can you imagine a mind state in which there is no bitter, condemning judgment of oneself or of others? This mind does not see the world in terms of good and bad, right and wrong, good and evil; it sees only "suffering and the end of suffering." What would happen if we looked at ourselves and all of the different things that we see and did not judge any of it? We would see that some things bring pain and others bring happiness, but there would be no denunciation, no guilt, no shame, no fear. How wondrous to see ourselves, others, and the world in that way! When we see only suffering and the end of suffering, then we feel compassion. Then we can act in energetic and forceful ways but without the corrosive effects of aversion.

Compassion can lead to very forceful action without any anger or aversion in it. When we see a small child reaching toward a hot burner on a stove, we instantly take action! Our response is born out of the compassion we feel: we move to pull the child back, away from harm. We do not reject or condemn the child.

To be compassionate is to wish that a being or all beings be free from pain. To be compassionate is to sense from within what it must be like to experience someone else's experience. I had such an opening at the end of my first visit to the Soviet Union. In the airport, just as I was leaving, I had to go through Soviet passport control. This inspection was done quite formally because, I imagine, they did not want Soviet citizens leaving the country with falsified foreign passports. So passport control was something of an ordeal. Smiling, I handed my passport to a uniformed Soviet official. He looked at my picture, and he looked at me, and he looked at my picture, and he looked at me. The look he gave me was, I think, the most hateful stare I have ever received from anybody in my life. It was an icy rage. It was the first time in my life that I had experienced that kind of energy so directly and personally. I just stood there, shocked. Finally, after quite a long period of time, the official handed me back my passport and told me to go.

I went to the transit lounge of the airport, where my traveling companions were waiting for me. I was very upset. I felt as though the man's energy had poisoned my being. I had absorbed his hatred, and I was reacting strongly to it. Then, in one moment, everything shifted. I thought, "If being exposed to his energy could make me feel so terrible after ten minutes, what would it be like to live inside that energetic vibration all the time?" I realized that this man might wake up, spend much of the day, and go to sleep in a state quite similar to the one I had just experienced from him. A tremendous feeling of compassion came into me for him. He was no longer a threatening enemy, but rather someone in what seemed to be intense suffering.

To view life compassionately, we have to look at what is happening and at the conditions that gave rise to it. Instead of only looking at the last point, or the end result, we need to see all of the constituent parts. The teachings of the Buddha can be distilled into an understanding that all things in the conditioned universe arise due to a cause. Have you ever had the experience of feeling resentful toward someone and then having an insight into what in their history might have caused them to behave in a certain way? Suddenly you can see the conditions that gave rise to that situation, not simply the end result of those conditions.

Once I knew two people, who had both suffered from abuse in childhood. One, a woman, grew up to be quite fearful, while the other, a man, grew up to be quite angry. The woman found herself in a work situation with the man, disliked him intensely, and was trying to have him fired from his job. At one point in the process, she got a glimpse into his background and recognized how they both had suffered in the same way. "He's a brother!" she exclaimed.

This kind of understanding does not mean that we dismiss or condone a person's negative behavior. But we can look at all of the elements that go into making up that person's life, and can acknowledge their conditioned nature. To see the interdependent arising of these impersonal forces that make up our "selves" can provide the opening for forgiveness and compassion.

Compassion means taking the time to look at the conditions, or the building blocks, of any situation. We must be able to look at things as they are actually arising in each moment. We must have the openness and spaciousness to see both the conditions and the context. We may, for example, hear a statement such as "Heroin is a very dangerous drug." This is undoubtedly true. But is it necessarily true for someone who is terminally ill, in excruciating pain? What is the context of the reality of the moment? If we can look in that way, we are not held to rigid categories that may close off our compassionate understanding.

How do we put compassion into action in our lives? The Buddha gave a teaching known as "the precious human birth," in which he described how rare and precious it is to take birth as a human in the vast cosmological scheme, and how as a human it is so rare and precious to experience just the right mixture of pleasure and pain to undertake deep spiritual inquiry. If there is too much pain in our lives, then we are overcome, perhaps needing to concentrate solely on how to survive each day. If there is too much pleasure, then we may get lazy and not have the motivating spark to look for meaning in our life.

This teaching fosters compassion in two ways. First, we can commit ourselves to creating for all others the kind of environment in which there is space and time enough for a spiritual opening, so that people can live according to the knowledge that they will die and find that truth which goes beyond this body and mind, which does not die. Second, if we see people, no matter what their worldly circumstances, squander the precious opportunity for awakening in this brief human life, we can be moved to compassion for them. Living with this awareness, every aspect of our lives can be an opportunity for compassion. Even a very simple action may be an extraordinary expression of the compassionate heart. Sometimes we think that to be compassionate we all have to be Mother Teresa. But we can look at the very simple things we do in our lives in order to see: What do they reflect about our relationship to pain? Do they reflect an understanding of pain? Are we looking at the various conditions making up a given situation, and are we looking at it in context?

Even very simple actions can make a big difference. We may not be able to take away the mass of somebody's suffering, but we can be present for them. Even if through our small act of being present, somebody does not feel as alone in their suffering as they once did, this will be a very great offering.

I was in a bad car accident in the late seventies. I arrived at Insight Meditation Society on crutches to teach a long retreat and I was having difficulty getting around. That was the year His Holiness the Dalai Lama came to visit. The preparations for his visit were intensive, because we had to arrange a great deal of security for this man who is considered a head of state. Our peaceful, rural retreat center became a stronghold. Pleasant Street was barricaded off, and state policemen patrolled the roof with guns. There were video cameras and a lot of excited activity. I was feeling dismal on crutches, especially when I ended up in the back of the huge crowd waiting to greet the Dalai Lama when he arrived. The car with His Holiness in it pulled up at last and was greeted by the cameras, the people, and the armed policemen. The Dalai Lama got out, looked around, and saw me standing way in the back of the throng, leaning on the crutches. He cut straight through the crowd and came up to me, as though he were homing in on the deepest suffering in the situation. He took my hand, looked me in the eye, and asked, "What happened?"

It was a beautiful moment. I had been feeling so left out. Now I suddenly felt so cared for. The Dalai Lama did not have to make the pain go away; in fact, he could not. But his simple acknowledgment, his openness, helped me feel included. Every act can be expressive of our deepest values.

Whatever life presents to us, our response can be an expression of our compassion. Whether someone speaks truthfully to us or deceitfully, harshly or gently, we might respond with a loving mind. This is also an act of compassionate service.

The Buddha himself expressed compassion in many different ways. His compassion was measureless, reaching from the most personal level to the most absolute. His service to beings ranged from caring for the sick to teaching a path of liberation. To him, the two were not distinct from each other.

Once a monk in the Buddha's time came down with a terrible disease that had some very unpleasant manifestations. He had, according to the text, oozing sores that looked and smelled so horrible that everybody avoided him completely. This monk lay helpless in bed, dying a grisly death with no one to care for him. When the Buddha became aware of this situation, he himself went into the monk's hut, bathed his wounds, cared for him, and gave him reassurance and spiritual instruction.

Later, the Buddha addressed the monastic community, saying that if somebody wanted to serve him, the Buddha, they should look after the sick. Those words seem so like ones spoken nearly five hundred years later by another compassionate spiritual teacher: "Whatsoever you do unto the least of these, so also you do unto me."

According to the Buddha, to develop compassion it is important to consider the human condition on every level: personal, social, and political. Once the Buddha described a king who decided to give over his kingdom to his son. He instructed him to be both righteous and generous in his new role as king. As time went on, although the new king took care to be just, he neglected to be generous. People became much poorer in his kingdom, and thievery increased. The king tried to suppress this thievery by instituting many harsh punishments. In commenting on this story, the Buddha pointed out how unsuccessful these punishments were. He went on to say that in order to suppress crime, the economic conditions of the people needed to be improved. He talked about how grain and agricultural help should be provided for farmers, capital should be given to traders, and adequate wages should be given to those who are employed.

Rather than responding to social problems through taxation or punishment, the Buddha's advice was to see the conditions that have come together to create a context in which people behave in a certain way, and then to change those conditions. The text states that poverty is one root of theft and violence, and that kings (or governments) must look at such causes in order to understand the effects. It is much easier to be moral if one's life is secure in some way, and much more difficult to refrain from stealing if one's children or parents are hungry. Thus our commitment should be to create conditions so that people can more easily be moral. The very pragmatism of this teaching of the Buddha reflects the depth of his compassion.

The Buddha's teaching is never removed from a sense of humanity. He described the motivating principle of his life as dedication to the welfare and the happiness of all beings, out of sympathy for all that lives. He also encouraged the same dedication in others: to see our very lives as vehicles to bring happiness, to bring peace, for the benefit of all beings.

This teaching dictates no particular expression of compassion. You can take up your umbrella with all the lovingkindness in your heart and hit somebody over the head. Or you may renounce the worldly life and live as a monastic, which does not mean renouncing love for all beings or a feeling of connectedness. There are many possibilities. A compassionate act does not have to be grandiose. The very simple action of love, of opening to people, of offering somebody some food, of saying hello, of asking what happened, of really being present—all are very powerful expressions of compassion. Compassion enjoins us to respond to pain, and wisdom guides the skillfulness of the response, telling us when and how to respond. Through compassion our lives become an expression of all that we understand and care about and value.

To develop a compassionate heart is not just an idealistic overlay. It arises from seeing the truth of suffering and opening to it. Out of this arises a sense of purpose, a sense of meaning so strong in our lives that no matter what the circumstances, no matter what the situation, our goal or our greatest desire at any moment is to express genuine love. Our inherent capacity for love can never be destroyed. Just as the whole earth cannot be destroyed by someone repeatedly hurling themselves against it, so too a compassionate heart will not be destroyed in an onslaught of adversity. Through practicing the brahma-vihara of compassion, we develop a mind that is vast and free from enmity. This is boundless, unconditioned love.

EXERCISE

Meditation on Compassion

In doing meditation specifically designed to nurture compassion, we usually use just one or two phrases, such as "May you be free of your pain and sorrow" or "May you find peace." It is important that the phrase be meaningful to you. Sometimes people feel more comfortable using a phrase that implies the wish for a more loving acceptance of pain, rather than freedom from pain. You should experiment with different phrases, seeing which ones support a compassionate opening to pain and which ones seem to lead you more in the direction of aversion or grief.

The first object of the compassion meditation is someone with great physical or mental suffering. The texts state that this should be a real person, not just a symbolic aggregate of all suffering beings. Spend some time directing the compassion phrase toward this person, remaining cognizant of their difficulties and heartaches.

You can progress from there through the same sequence that unfolds in the metta practice: self, benefactor, friend, neutral person, difficult person, all beings, all living beings, . . . all females, all males, . . . all beings in the ten directions.

Take up the compassion practice at your own pace—move from category to category as you feel ready. Remember that all beings face great potential suffering, no matter how fortunate their immediate circumstance might be. This is simply the nature of change in the course of life's unfolding.

If you feel yourself moving from the trembling of the heart that is compassion into states of fear, despair, or sorrow, first of all accept that this is natural. Breathe softly, and use your awareness of the breath to anchor yourself in this moment. Reach underneath the fear or rejection of pain to the sense of oneness with all beings that underlies it. You can reflect on that sense of oneness and rejoice in it.

Suffering is an intrinsic part of life and will certainly not disappear from the lives of beings no matter how earnestly we wish for it to. What we are doing in the compassion meditation is purifying and transforming our relationship to suffering, whether it is our own or that of others. Being able to acknowledge suffering, open to it, and respond to it with a tenderness of heart allows us to join with all beings, and to realize that we are never alone.

EXERCISE
Compassion for Those Who Cause Pain

A further compassion meditation begins with using the phrase "May you be free of your pain and sorrow," directed toward someone who is causing harm in the world. This is based on the understanding that causing harm to others inevitably means creating harm for oneself, both now and in the future. Seeing someone lie, steal, or hurt beings in some other way is therefore the ground out of which compassion for them can arise. When I've taught this meditation on retreats, people often choose their least favorite political leader as the object. It is not necessarily an easy practice, but it can revolutionize our understanding.

If you are filled with judgment or condemnation of yourself or others, can you revise your perceptions to see the world in terms of suffering and the end of suffering, instead of good and bad? To see the world in terms of suffering and the end of suffering is buddha-mind, and will lead us away from righteousness and anger. Get in touch with your own buddha-mind, and you will uncover a healing force of compassion.

You can move from directing compassion to someone creating harm, through the cycle of beings (self, benefactor, etc.). Notice particularly whether this meditation, over time, creates a different relationship to yourself, and to your enemy. Remember that compassion doesn't need to justify itself—it is its own reason for being.

8

Liberating the Mind through Sympathetic Joy

In a battle, the winners and the losers both lose.
—*The Buddha*

I<small>T IS A RARE</small> and beautiful quality to feel truly happy when others are happy. When someone rejoices in our happiness, we are flooded with respect and gratitude for their appreciation. When we take delight in the happiness of another, when we genuinely rejoice at their prosperity, success, or good fortune rather than begrudging it in any way, we are abiding in mudita, sympathetic joy, the third of the four brahma-viharas, or boundless states of consciousness.

The root of the Pali word *mudita* means "to be pleased, to have a sense of gladness." The Buddha called mudita "the mind-deliverance of gladness," because this force of happiness actually liberates us. Unlike a state of mere excitement or giddiness, the quality of sympathetic joy challenges our deep assumptions about aloneness, loss, and happiness, and shows us another possibility. It defeats many of the qualities of consciousness that bind us.

So much of our unhappy condition as living beings comes from the constricting effect of our negativity toward each other. We limit ourselves, and we limit others. We judge each other, compare ourselves to each other, demean and envy each other, and we ourselves suffer the strangling effects of these limitations. Because there are so many constricting mind states that are impediments to mudita, sympathetic joy is considered the most difficult of all the brahma-viharas to develop. But so potent is this quality that expressing it can defeat the aversion and attachment that bind us.

The Buddhist scriptures tell a wonderful parable about a kind of monkey trap. To make the trap, some tar is spread on the ground. A monkey then comes along and steps in the sticky tar. First one little monkey foot gets stuck. In trying to free itself, the monkey puts down another foot. Then it puts down one hand, then the other hand. Finally, in a desperate effort to gain some leverage and free itself, the monkey puts down its head. That is a very stuck monkey!

That is just how those tormenting states of mind, such as judging, comparing, discriminating, demeaning, and envying, collude to get us stuck, to keep us stuck, and to make us miserable. When that monkey has just one foot in the tar, instead of putting down the next foot and then the hands, if it were to reach out and grab a tree and pull itself away, it could be free. Mudita can provide just that kind of opportunity to extricate ourselves from our stuckness, to be free enough from the tar traps in our lives to be happy. If we look carefully at each of those mind states where we get stuck, we can begin to understand how cultivating sympathetic joy can help to free us.

Judgment

It is all too easy to believe, or even insist, that other people should behave just as we want them to, that they should pursue lifestyles and sources of happiness in precisely the ways we deem appropriate. With this orientation, no wonder we find it difficult to be happy for the countless people we can never control. We may feel disgruntled and frustrated with others as they simply go about living their lives.

To be nonjudgmental means having flexibility of mind and the ability to let go of our attachment to what seems right to us. Have you ever had the experience of giving someone advice or offering an opinion that turned out to be drastically wrong? For example, someone you know is about to go on vacation to a particular place where you had a difficult time. You say, "Don't go there. It's inconvenient, the weather is bad, the people are unfriendly. If you go, you're going to end up miserable!"

But she goes there anyway and has a wonderful time. Can you let go of having given that terribly mistaken piece of advice and simply say, "I'm delighted that you had a good time"? How many times are we wrong? Perhaps quite a few times in any given day! And if we see that someone has ignored our advice and has come out very well nonetheless, can we be happy for them? Can we uphold another's happiness as a priority over our own righteousness?

Sympathetic joy is nonjudgmental; it slices through our predilection to force the world to accord with our views. People may choose to live in ways quite different from our lives. They may do things differently from how we do them. They may find happiness in things that would not bring much happiness to us personally. Some may choose to live more comfortably, while we may choose to live more simply. Some may have children, while we may choose not to. Can we allow the lives of others to be different from ours and feel happy for them? Can we rejoice for them as their happiness grows, in whatever way that is happening?

Of course, a certain element of discernment is important here as well. People may delude themselves into thinking they are doing something that will bring them happiness, when they are actually creating unhappiness for themselves or for others. Sympathetic joy does not mean that whenever someone proclaims their happiness, we are delighted. Sometimes we might perceive that they are actually miserable, or setting themselves up to be. But if people are genuinely happy in their choice of action or lifestyle, we do not need to impose our standards. If they are not harming themselves, if they are not harming others, can we be generous enough to feel joy for them? That is the practice of mudita.

Comparing

Comparing ourselves to others is a very powerful mental affliction. In Buddhist psychology it is called "conceit." When we are enmeshed in conceit, we are pulled outside ourselves, trying to know who we are and what our experience is by comparing ourselves to others. "Who am I in reference to that? Am I good enough in comparison to that?" Whether we conclude that we are better than, worse than, or equal to another, when we measure ourselves against others, it causes us harm. As we constantly try to decide, through comparison with others, who we are, what is important about us, whether or not we are happy, that churning of the mind in itself undermines our happiness.

Comparison or conceit is a gnawing, painful restlessness. It can never bring us to peace, because there is no end to the possibilities for comparison. You may be sitting in a room, for example, and you notice that the person sitting near you is quite attractive. He also seems articulate. So your first conclusion is, "Well, I'm not as good-looking as that one." Then you notice that the person in front of you looks somewhat drab and worn out. Perhaps he seems to be struggling for words as he tries to express himself. You think, "Oh, good. I'm better than this one. I'm smarter and look better." But then you may feel a nagging doubt: "What if he's been working all night in a computer lab making breakthroughs in research, while I can barely use my word processor? Maybe I'm not as good as he is, after all." By the time you have more or less established your status in reference to everyone around you, someone new arrives, and the anxious comparing begins all over again.

At the center of the comparing mind is competition. Who is going to win by being better? The Buddha once said, "In a battle, the winners and the losers both lose." The defeated lose power, freedom, property, family, and sometimes their lives. But the winners of the battle find themselves left with the hatred, fear, and envy of those who have been overcome. In the cycle of revenge, it is just a matter of time until the wheel turns, and those who have been winners become losers. When the battle is an inner one, over who is inherently better or worse, who is happier and more deserving, we are setting ourselves up to lose.

In practicing sympathetic joy rather than looking at others in order to define ourselves, we begin by recognizing that we do indeed deserve to be happy. Out of that confidence we are able to delight in the happiness of others instead of feeling threatened by it. Rather than losing ourselves in the centrifugal force of longing that pulls our focus outward toward what we think we don't have, sympathetic joy reorients our relationship to the world into one of opening and effortless giving.

Prejudice

When someone we love experiences loss, blame, or conflict, we can easily feel angry and upset. We can also feel anger when someone we do not like experiences prosperity or praise or happiness in their lives. Imagine sitting in a room and listening while a lot of people heap praise upon some person you don't like. How awful to be in that situation! Imagine the rage that could come up, the hostility. But can you also imagine even the possibility of actually feeling some joy that that person whom you do not like is experiencing a moment of happiness?

The willingness to feel goodwill only toward those we like is a powerful impediment to developing sympathetic joy. Crossing that line of discrimination, from people we like to people we dislike, can be very difficult. I encountered this when I was first doing intensive metta practice in Burma and was asked to direct metta toward an "enemy" or person I had difficulty with in my life. When done with strong concentration, we were being taught, metta can reach the person it is being directed toward. If he or she is open to receive it, metta can actually provide them some comfort and happiness. As I sat there, trying to decide which one to choose as my "difficult person," I found myself thinking, "Better not choose that person. What if I get really concentrated, and he starts to feel better based on my metta? I don't want him to feel better—that's why he is in the category of difficult people to begin with. Better to choose this other one. But wait, there is the exact same problem with her!" I finally had to laugh as I confronted how I was holding on to whatever happiness I might purportedly be able to bestow, and the anxiety it was causing me.

Like metta, mudita is boundless. As it develops in us, we are able to rejoice in the happiness and well-being of others, whether we like them or not. It is through compassion that we begin to extend sympathetic joy beyond our prejudices. Compassion reminds us that everyone suffers. Since that is true, do we really want some person whom we do not like to experience only more and more suffering? Should they have only pain in ever-increasing amounts until the day they die? What would such a wish mean in terms of what we value in our minds and hearts? Remembering the truth of the vast potential for suffering in this world, we can feel happy that someone, anyone, also experiences some happiness. As Henry Wadsworth Longfellow said, "If we could read the secret history of our enemies we should find in each man's life sorrow and suffering enough to disarm all hostility." Everyone's life is by nature continually vulnerable to pain. Remembering this is our gateway to mudita.

Demeaning

Another definition of practicing mudita is to be nondemeaning. We may look at someone else's achievements or someone else's happiness and find ourselves wishing that their status or condition might be diminished—as if thereby our own would be increased. This attitude of diminishing the happiness of others is based on considering happiness as a limited resource or commodity—the more someone else has, the less there is for me.

This perspective, so common in regard to material things or objects, can also arise in relation to qualities like love, faith, or joy. We might be resentful of someone who has a great deal of faith or love, someone who can feel basically at ease even when they are encountering hard times or who can exhibit kindness in the face of difficulty. Besides feeling as if we might not be able to have as much faith or love, because they've already got it all, we can also suffer by feeling that we fall short by comparison and want to diminish them so that they are more like us.

When we view reality in that way—the more someone else has, the less we can have—then certainly it is easy to feel the threat of deprivation, to become resentful and embittered, and to feel the need to demean others. When we feel that there is a fixed or static amount of good things in life, we must constantly compete for them. When we have no concept of the ability of good qualities to flower and replenish themselves, we are all impoverished.

In the classical tradition of Buddhism, the practice of "sharing merit" counteracts the delusion and damage of such limited benefits. We accrue merit through acting in ways that are helpful and beneficial to others. However, it is not as if we are piling up the benefits of our good deeds in a warehouse somewhere. Merit is a force that is far more dynamic and subtle than that. It is a power that is born in and grows through acts of goodness.

There is an energetic consequence to what we think about and care about and do, and we can perceive it. When we give something to someone, there is a tangible power in that action. When we comfort someone in pain, when we give of our time, when we meditate, we can sense a genuine force in the moment of performing the action. When we have insight into the true nature of things, when we offer something out of care, when we develop a loving heart, we are engaged in meritorious actions.

The energy that we feel in this way we can dedicate to the well-being of others. This is the sharing of merit. One traditional recitation in the practice is: "May the merit of this action be shared by all beings everywhere, so that they may come to the end of suffering." We may share merit with any individual, any group, or all beings without exception. Traditionally people share merit with someone who has died, so that the deceased can benefit from that liberating energy.

Sharing merit is itself a potent, wholesome action that generates its own considerable power. Buddhist teachings say that when you offer your merit to others, your own merit grows. By giving this energy away, you get more! I used to consider that concept and wonder, "Well, how does it do that? I just gave it away. How does it grow?" By analogy, it is easy to see how that occurs with happiness. Happiness does not go away when we share it. It is not a limited commodity that has to be somehow rationed out and conserved very carefully so as not to deplete our supply. It grows simply because the act of sharing puts us in touch with its source, which is limitless.

Demeaning the good fortune of others is a self-defeating strategy. Wishing to diminish the happiness of others only diminishes our own. Likewise, augmenting the happiness of others, even of people we do not like, augments our own. There is no boundary to happiness; there is no end.

Envy

Envy, as we all know to our distress, is the inability to endure the success, prosperity, or happiness of others; it absolutely hates to see these things in other people. The experience of envy only functions to produce more and more dissatisfaction with our own condition and to make us quite miserable. In English, we use the phrase "eaten up by envy." That says it all. Envy devours us. We cease to be centered within our own lives, but instead are perpetually out of balance as we lean into the lives of others, regretting their happiness, real or imagined.

In the difficulties of my early meditation practice, when I was sleepy and restless and uncertain, I would often peek at other meditators to see how they were doing. I would see them with their eyes closed, silent and unmoving, and I was sure that they were all sitting in great bliss. Why wasn't I? The feelings of deprivation were quite strong in me. I felt like an impoverished child with my nose pressed up against a bakery window, destined to be excluded from the riches within. I was truly eaten up with envy. The irony of it all, as I learned later, was that while I was imagining the unmitigated success of others, these other meditators in turn were feeling envy for what they imagined my extraordinary experience to be!

Envy is often based on such illusion. It is a very destructive quality, and if it grows to be very strong, then it is easy for us to try to hurt someone toward whom we feel envious. In the end, we only hurt ourselves. How much easier to simply be happy for the happiness of others, knowing that this gives rise to our own.

Avarice

Avarice or selfishness is a quality whereby one seeks to hold on to and conceal what one has in order to avoid sharing it with others. In the presence of avarice, sharing is impossible. Avarice manifests as meanness and contraction in the mind, and is characterized by extreme possessiveness and attachment. It does not want others to hear or know about something that is bringing us happiness, lest we have to share it with anyone.

We may feel avarice in relation to a variety of objects: friends, material things, learning, ideas, attributes such as intelligence or beauty. When this desire to possess something exclusively is powerful enough, we begrudge those who have the same quality. We want no one else to have what we have. In team teaching, such as the Western teachers of my tradition tend to do, I am often afforded the interesting experience of hearing a colleague use an apt quotation I myself had unearthed, or telling a story I was planning on using in my discourse the very next night. It is remarkable to see myself wanting to hoard wisdom, as though it were a commodity anyone could selectively own.

Avarice causes tremendous pain. There is no peace in it. In this state we are constantly looking around, on guard to hide what we have so that no one else can experience its benefits, and we are miserable when we find someone who does. The roots of envy and avarice are aversion toward others and attachment to objects, both material and abstract. The gladness which is the essence of sympathetic joy uproots envy and avarice as the mind fills with the qualities of delight and appreciation for others and the wish for them to be happy.

Boredom

Mudita is also said to eliminate boredom. The first time I read this claim, I wondered, "How could sympathetic joy overcome boredom?" I came to the conclusion that mudita eliminates boredom because it gives us so many reasons to feel happy and connected. Boredom is based on a sense of separateness and a turning away that we feel when we experience certain degrees of aversion. When we stop paying attention to the little things in life, and the little things in our meditation practice as well, we find ourselves in a state of boredom.

By reconnecting to the little things, we awaken again to a delightful kind of openness. Taking the time to marvel at a little flower as it creeps up through a crack in the pavement, we can feel joy, even though we are aware that this planet is in a very severe ecological crisis. Despite the venality, hatred, and monstrous egoism evident in some human actions, remembering the fortitude, courage, and love people are capable of can awaken our appreciation. When we are touched by things, moved by the actions of people, we open to what is around us. When we feel happy for others, we feel happy and connected ourselves. The separation and dullness of boredom is dissolved.

To be able to notice the less obvious beauty, to appreciate it, to change perspective for a time is a type of quiet, a way of rest. We do this by being fully aware in the moment. If we simply feel the miracle of being present, a kind of appreciation grows along with a kind of joy. Attending to the small things in front of us becomes a way of self-renewal and self-refreshment.

Allies of Mudita

The impediments to mudita—judgment, comparing, discriminating, demeaning, envy, avarice, boredom—all are rooted in the binding forces of aversion and attachment. By contrast, qualities that support mudita—rapture, gratitude, metta, compassion—share their origin in our basic goodness, and they form a potent team to reduce suffering and to bring happiness.

Mudita depends on rapture, on our capacity to take active delight in things—and this depends upon our ability to actually let ourselves feel joy. We have to let go of feeling guilt about our own happiness or feeling threatened that it will be taken from us. When we hoard our pleasure or happiness, we feel disdainful of other people and their suffering. At times, we may feel disdainful of ourselves and our own suffering as well. But it is essential that we take delight in our own happiness as a perfect expression of our basic motivation to be free.

We gladden the mind because that helps free us. When we remember the good things we have done, the times of generosity and caring, the times of holding back from hurting someone, we can rejoice in our own goodness. We do good because it frees the heart. It opens us to a wellspring of happiness. We can begin to view our aspirations in this light. We aspire to good in order to grow, to yield, to become more and more open, more connected, to be happy ourselves, and thus happy for others.

Another ally of mudita is gratitude. Gratitude brings delight. The phrase "Count your blessings" has become a kind of sentimental cliché in our society, and yet there is wisdom in it. So important did the Buddha consider counting our blessings that he specifically detailed many of them in the discourse called the *Mangala Sutta*. (*Mangala* means "blessing" in Pali.) In it he talks about blessings that can be enjoyed by any one of us if we create the conditions for them: to live a just life; to have a good home life; to have a livelihood or discipline we like and can perform well; to honor contentedness and gratitude; to have a sense of patience. One important blessing he notes is having good friends, being able to associate with wise and good-hearted people. If we want to strengthen qualities such as wisdom, equanimity, concentration, rapture, or mudita, spending time with those who have those qualities supports them in us.

An even greater blessing is to be in a situation where we can discuss the Dharma, or the truth. Then far greater than that is to be able to live the Dharma. And then to see the truth for ourselves, to have a realization of the cessation of suffering, is a supreme blessing. We are profoundly blessed when we have a mind that remains unshaken when it is touched by all of the changes of the world—all of the joys and sorrows as they continually fluctuate. This is what the Buddha called the greatest happiness: to know peace unchanged by changing conditions.

When one moves on a spiritual path, one is moving in an ocean of blessings. The Buddha said that "such a one goes everywhere with safety." Contemplating the possibility of such blessings and such safety is itself a source of happiness. So counting our blessings cultivates gratitude and happiness in us, which opens us to joy when others are blessed.

Compassion is an ally which mutually complements mudita. Just as mudita reminds us of joy when we are lost in sorrow, compassion reminds us of pain when we are lost in denial. Compassion balances sympathetic joy and keeps it from degenerating into sentimentality or ignorant optimism. Mudita keeps compassion from degenerating into brooding over the enormous breadth, depth, and duration of suffering in the world. It gives solace to the compassionate heart so that we do not feel flooded or overwhelmed by pain.

Compassion guards mudita, and mudita guards compassion. Together in their complementary ways the two keep us from building barriers behind which we confine ourselves to experiencing only a narrow segment of life. And because mudita energizes us, it also helps compassion to be active. We can take the joy of the mudita and use it to help translate our inner experience of compassion into an outward act of service in the world.

When we open to the suffering of beings, the joy at the heart of compassion complements the joy of mudita that arises when we open to their happiness. It seems strange that we can feel joy in the face of pain, but that is what happens. Compassion brings us closer to others. The power of harmony, of union, that grows in the heart from being close to one in pain infuses compassion with openness, tenderness, concentration, and bliss. And so we can feel happiness whether we respond to the joy of beings or to their suffering.

As mudita grows, we see that the happiness of others is our happiness. They are not different. Thus mudita strengthens metta. Sympathetic joy allows us to open further and further with lovingkindness, so that more and more we really do want other people to be happy. The happiness of another, even an "enemy's" happiness, is not going to take away from us in any way. In truth, our happiness and that of others is inseparable.

Mudita along with compassion and metta are all engaged in a powerful dance of mutual support. The selflessness and boundless nature of metta enables us to extend the feelings of compassion or sympathetic joy not only to those we know but also to those we do not know. We proffer our openness of heart not just to those who are suffering but also to those who are happy, and not just to those who are happy but also to those who are suffering. We wish for beings whomever they are that they be free from danger and pain, that they be peaceful and happy.

So these three brahma-viharas all add to one another. Theirs is a benevolent alliance to brighten our minds. And because of their brightness, they add richness and joy to our perceptions. We can increasingly open to the happiness that exists. And we can see the suffering that exists as well and maintain an open heart in the face of it. In this way, as they share their strengths with one another, the bright forces of mind support us and help us to our own happiness.

EXERCISE

Meditation on Sympathetic Joy

As we undertake sympathetic joy as a formal meditation practice, we begin with someone whom we care about; someone it is easy to rejoice for. It may be somewhat difficult even then, but we tend to more easily feel joy for someone on the basis of our love and friendship. Choose a friend and focus on a particular gain or source of joy in this person's life. Do not look for absolute, perfect happiness in their life, because you may not find it. Whatever good fortune or happiness of theirs comes to your mind, take delight in it with the phrase "May your happiness and good fortune not leave you" or "May your happiness not diminish" or "May your good fortune continue." This will help diminish the conditioned tendencies of conceit, demeaning others, and judgment.

Following this, we move through the sequence of beings: benefactor, neutral person, enemy, all beings, . . . all beings in the ten directions.

The relationship between sympathetic joy and compassion figures more strongly as we direct sympathetic joy toward someone who is suffering a great deal. Can we find within their life some little happiness, something that is bringing them satisfaction, or faith, or maybe just an opening for changing a circumstance that is causing them pain? If we can focus on *any* auspicious feature in their life, and then rejoice over that, we can be practicing sympathetic joy even toward those who are in great pain.

If you cannot find anything at all to rejoice over, send sympathetic joy as best as possible, to purify your own mind of the tendencies toward envy or jealousy. Sometimes we can feel compassion for someone when they are down, but we actually resent it if their fortunes change, and we no longer feel as secure in relationship to them.

Traditionally, sympathetic joy is practiced in sympathy with others, not in terms of oneself. What is essential to develop in terms of oneself are the abilities to rejoice and to have gratitude. Remember the reflection on good things you have done, or acts of generosity you have performed—it is important to be able to take delight in these, and to be able to distinguish that delight from conceit. Remember the reflection on the good within you, and the rightness of your wish to be happy, along with your understanding of a path to happiness—this is a source of exceptional gratitude.

EXERCISE
Sharing Merit

At the end of an act of generosity, or meditation, or anything wholesome, you can share the potency of the act with anyone you choose—someone who has died, a friend who is suffering, or all beings everywhere without distinction. Feel the positive energy of the action, and dedicate it: "May the merit of this action be shared by all beings, so that they may be liberated." Dedicate it in whatever way is meaningful to you. We share the merit as an acknowledgment that our spiritual work is never really for ourselves alone. Whatever our beliefs, it could never be for ourselves alone, and this is one way of remembering that.

9

The Gift of Equanimity

All beings are the owners of their karma. Their happiness and unhappiness depend on their actions, not on my wishes for them.

Some years ago Joseph Goldstein and I went to Calcutta to visit one of our teachers, Dipa Ma. She was elderly, and it seemed important to see her as soon as possible. As it happened, the only time we could visit was between teaching retreats, on our way from one in Sweden to another in Australia. That meant we would arrive in India during the monsoon season. The day after we got there, we went straight to Dipa Ma's home and stayed with her for the day. Outside it was raining torrentially, but I was so happy to be with Dipa Ma again that I paid no attention to the tremendous downpour.

When we left her at dusk and went down to the street, we discovered what happens in Calcutta after a long period of torrential rain: the sewers flood, overflow, and pour through the streets. Sewage mixed with rainwater was flowing, perhaps three feet deep, past the front of the house. We stood on the step, looking at that extraordinary scene. Since cabs and rickshaws couldn't move through such a flood, we would have to walk back to our hotel. Joseph, who is quite a bit taller than I am, commented, "This should be interesting!" I thought, "Well, yes, if you're six-foot-three it may be interesting. If you're my height, this is not going to be so interesting!"

We stepped off into the flood. It was absolutely horrible to be wading through that: the depth of it, the stench, things brushing against my legs in the twilight. When the sewers overflow in

Calcutta, the rats are forced out as well, and they filled the streets. Desperate, drowning rats bumped against my legs as we sloshed along. All of my senses, including my mind, were being assaulted by terrible, vile experiences.

Four or five days later we arrived in Australia. A friend had gotten us tickets to a symphony at the Sydney Opera House, which is a splendid architectural marvel built right on the ocean harbor. Before the concert, she took us out to dinner at one of those elegant restaurants that perch high above a city and revolve as you eat. Sydney is a very beautiful place, and we enjoyed lovely, sweeping vistas of it as we savored the meal of many delicious and well-presented courses. At the concert everyone was clean, smelling very nice and beautifully dressed. As we sat there listening to the wonderful music of Dvořák and Brahms, taking in pleasures through every sense door, I remembered Calcutta. What had happened to that reality?

The next time this friend and I shared a meal was six months later in Burma, where we were practicing meditation at a monastery. We sat at the same table during the retreat. All the food at such practice centers is donated by laypeople who revere meditation practice. The Burmese are a notably generous people, but most of them are also very poor, so the food they offer, though it is the best they can afford, can also be quite poor. It can also be, as is customary in Burma, quite oily. That was the case on that particular day. The main course was a bitter vegetable floating in four or five inches of oil. As you chewed this vegetable, it turned into a ball of wooden pulp in your mouth. This meal, our main sustenance for that day, was meager and seemed almost inedible. As my friend offered me the serving dish to see if I wanted seconds, I remembered that last meal she and I had shared, in the ever-so-lovely revolving restaurant in Sydney, with the elegant service, the exquisite food, and the panorama of that beautiful city. Where was that reality now?

In six months, even in one day or one hour, we can experience so many extremes of pleasure and pain. The question is, how can a human heart—my heart or your heart—absorb the continual, unremitting contrasts of this life without feeling shattered and thinking that we cannot bear it? Battered by changes, the heart-mind can become brittle, rigid. It can wither and shrink. The Buddha said that our hearts can wilt as a flower does when it has been out in the sun too long. Have you ever encountered this feeling?

How can we live with such vicissitudes? How can we hold them all with some sense of wholeness, coherence, harmony? Can we actually experience freedom in the midst of all of these immense changes, as they roll through our lives over and over again? Can we actually be happy in this continuous arising and passing away?

When we introduce the practice of metta meditation, we ask the students to evoke their deepest aspirations, the things they want most for themselves in life. Sometimes it is quite difficult to know what is the best we would offer ourselves. Do we want comfort? Do we want excitement? Do we want freedom? Do we want security? What do we want most fundamentally in this life, and do we achieve it through trying to control the endless change of circumstance, or do we achieve it through learning to let go? The practice of equanimity is learning deeply what it means to let go.

The four boundless states that we call the brahma-viharas or divine abodes culminate with equanimity. In Pali equanimity is called *upekkha*, which means "balance," and its characteristic is to arrest the mind before it falls into extremes. Equanimity is a spacious stillness of the mind, a radiant calm that allows us to be present fully with all the different changing experiences that constitute our world and our lives.

When we look carefully at our experience, both internal and external, we see that change is fundamental, intrinsic to the entire living world. Outside ourselves we see alternating rhythms of photosynthesis and the respiration of plants. Within ourselves we see the rhythms of our own biochemistry. Everything is moving, vibrating, pulsating in rhythm. These alternations are also found within the rhythms of the planet, in the ebb and flow of tides, the cycles of night and day and of the seasons, and all the cycles of the natural world.

When we look at our own lives, we see extraordinary patterns of flow and movement. Think for a moment about what series of circumstances brought you to be sitting in the particular place where you are now, reading this book. So many different changing events and experiences have led to this moment and this action. At the time they happened, some of those experiences may have seemed very unfortunate, and yet in some way they had a role in this pattern that brought you here to this distinct time and place. Thus we see that life is not really a series of unanchored, chaotic events. Rather, it is like a mosaic; it has a pattern. Each experience has some part in creating the whole. We can see harmony in the bigger picture.

In the staff dining room at Insight Meditation Society, we have a big collage of baby photos on the wall. They are baby pictures of those of us who were at IMS during the first five years or so. Sometimes I am amazed to contemplate how all of those little beings, with all of their different circumstances, surroundings, and conditioning, ended up together in that one place serving as staff or teachers or board members. It is extraordinary to consider the complex flow of changing events that made this convergence possible.

One day over lunch we discovered that one staff member at IMS had been attending the University of California at Berkeley in the sixties, during the student riots, and someone else on the same staff had been a policeman in Berkeley at that very same time! How remarkable to think that these two people, who may have encountered each other from their separate sides during the riots, would come together again so many years later in such very different conditions to share a common purpose. This remarkable flow of experience is the great tapestry of our lives.

Sometimes, of course, it is hard to embrace the painful, difficult times as being part of that whole, to feel as connected to those harsh events as we do when things are pleasant, easy, and fortunate. But really our lives are composed of continual change without ceasing. What the ancient Taoists called "the ten thousand joys and the ten thousand sorrows" come and go over and over again. As the Buddha said, pleasure and pain, gain and loss, praise and blame, fame and disrepute constantly arise and pass away, beyond our control.

One of my friends who leads meditation retreats honors the Asian habit, as I do, of bowing to the image of the Buddha when he enters the meditation hall at the beginning of sittings. After one sitting, he told me, he received two notes from students who had been in the hall with him. One note said, "I saw you bowing to the Buddha, and I was really offended. It is rank superstition, and it has no place here. You should stop doing it." The other note said, "I saw you bowing to the Buddha, and I want you to know that it was the most moving thing that has ever happened to me here. It made all the difference in my retreat. I am so grateful that you did it."

That is just how it is: we act, hopefully out of the best intentions we can find within us, and at times we receive praise, and at times we receive blame. There is a story in Buddhist teachings that illustrates this point well. One day a man visited the Buddha's monastery, seeking some knowledge of the teachings. The first monk he came upon was deep in silent meditation and did not answer when the man spoke to him. The visitor became enraged and stomped away. The next day he came back and happened upon a learned, erudite disciple, who responded to his question about the teachings with a lengthy, intricate discourse. Once again the man became furious and went off. He came back again the next day and chanced upon the Buddha's disciple Ananda.

Now, Ananda had heard what had happened on the first day, when the monk said nothing at all, and what had happened on the second day, when the monk replied at great length, so he was very careful to deliver only a medium-length discourse—something, but not something so very long. Amazingly, the visitor once more became enraged. He said to Ananda, "How dare you treat such weighty matters so sketchily?" and for the final time he ran away.

When the monks approached the Buddha and described what had happened on each of these three days, the Buddha wisely replied: "There is always blame in this world. If you say too much, some people will blame you. If you say a little bit, some people will blame you. If you say nothing at all, some people will blame you."

This is the very nature of life. No one in this world experiences only pleasure and no pain, and no one experiences only gain and no loss. When we open to this truth, we discover that there is no need to hold on or to push away. Rather than trying to control what can never be controlled, we can find a sense of security in being able to meet what is actually happening. This is allowing for the mystery of things: not judging but rather cultivating a balance of mind that can receive what is happening, whatever it is. This acceptance is the source of our safety and confidence.

When we feel unhappiness or pain, it is not a sign that things have gone terribly wrong or that we have done something wrong by not being able to control the circumstances. Pain and pleasure are constantly coming and going, and yet we can be happy. When we allow for the mystery, sometimes we discover that right in the heart of a very difficult time, right in the midst of a painful situation, there is freedom. In those moments when we realize how much we cannot control, we can learn to let go.

As we begin to understand this, we move from a mode of struggling to control what comes into our lives into a mode of simply wishing to truly connect with what is. This is a radical shift in worldview.

Normally we live with a level of denial that deadens us. A friend once related this story: His father was a young child, driving with his own father in a car on December 7, 1941. A sudden announcement came over the car radio, "The Japanese have attacked Pearl Harbor!" Immediately my friend's grandfather leaned over and said urgently to his son, "Don't tell your mother!" When hearing this I thought, "Right, maybe he hoped she wouldn't notice any of World War II." When we define more and more experiences as unacceptable to feel or to know, life becomes smaller and smaller; it gets very limited. When we become willing to experience everything, the confidence and certainty we once sought by denying change we can find by embracing it. We learn to relate to life fully, including the insecurity.

Part of this full relationship is a careful examination of our reality. The Buddha talked about the six ways in which we experience the world, the six doors of perception: through seeing, hearing, smelling, tasting, touching, and through the mind door by thinking, feeling emotions, and seeing mental images. Those six ways of perceiving define the totality of our experience. The Buddha went on to say that every single moment of being alive, which involves one of these six experiences, has a feeling tone to it. So in every moment we experience pleasure, pain, or neutrality.

For instance, we see an object, and in that moment our experience is pleasurable, it is unpleasant, or it is neutral. Then there immediately follows a reaction to that feeling. When the experience is pleasant and we do not want it to go away, we tend to cling with attachment. When we do not like the experience, when it is painful, we tend to react with aversion, by condemning or pushing away. Because we often depend on intense pleasure and pain for a sense of feeling awake or alive, when the experience is neutral, we tend to react by falling asleep, either literally or by lapsing into inattention. In Buddhism this is considered falling into delusion.

Most of the time, our hearts and minds respond to the ten thousand joys and ten thousand sorrows by careening back and forth, over and over again, between elation and despair, the violent movement for and against what our experience is. Or we respond with denial in its many manifestations: indifference, repression, not noticing, muffled anxiety, feeling disconnected.

Fortunately, as the Buddha revealed, rather than being lost in these conditioned reactions, we can learn to be balanced in response to them. Such balance does not mean that we do not feel things anymore. Meditation does not turn us into gray, vegetative blobs with all the feelings washed out. The Buddha taught that we can feel pleasure fully, yet without craving or clinging, without defining it as our ultimate happiness. We can feel pain fully without condemning or hating it. And we can experience neutral events by being fully present, so that they are not just fill-in times until something more exciting comes along. This nonreactivity is the state of equanimity, and it leads us into freedom in each moment.

Early in my meditation practice, when I was in India, one of my teachers often talked about this miracle of nonreactivity. As he spoke, extensive inner dialogues would be going on in me. "That is so inspiring! This is the most wonderful teaching I have ever heard, that in a single moment you can really experience freedom. If only I could get rid of this knee pain, I know that I could really go far with this practice!"

My teacher would continue, elaborating on the teaching, and my internal running commentary would continue along with it. "It's so amazing. I've never been so inspired by anything in my life! I must have been a Buddhist in a previous lifetime to have so much affinity with this teaching. If only I could get rid of this knee pain, I know that I could get enlightened so soon! Maybe I'll go down to that yoga ashram in South India. I'll really stretch out my body there. Then I won't have any more of this pain. I'll come back in six months, and then I can get enlightened!"

That stream of consciousness grew and grew, until one day, many months down the road, I woke up and realized that what my teacher was talking about, and what in fact the Buddha had been talking about, was my knee pain. Here was an unpleasant experience in the moment. How was I relating to it? Was there grasping or aversion or delusion? Or was there acceptance, letting go? Was there bondage or was there freedom?

Instead of waiting to trade in my present experience for something better in the future, I came back to opening to the pain just as it was and honoring it. I stopped seeing it as irrelevant, as a burden or a curse, and started seeing it as the truth of the moment. The Buddha's teaching is not remote or abstract; it is about our knee pain and how we respond to it right here. Krishnamurti once said, "Freedom is now or never."

Equanimity's strength derives from a combination of understanding and trust. It is based on understanding that the conflict and frustration we feel when we can't control the world doesn't come from our inability to do so but rather from the fact that we are trying to control the uncontrollable. We know better than to try to prevent the seasons from changing or the tide from coming in. Following autumn, winter comes. We may not prefer it, but we trust it because we understand and accept its rightful place in a larger cycle, a bigger picture. Can we apply the same wise balance to the cycles and tides of pleasant, unpleasant, and neutral experiences in our lives?

A Chinese poem expresses the essence of this trust and understanding:

> Ten thousand flowers in spring, the moon in autumn,
> A cool breeze in summer, snow in winter—
> If your mind is not clouded by unnecessary things,
> this is the best season of your life.

To see things as they are, to see the changing nature, to see the impermanence, to see that constant flow of pleasant and painful events outside our control—that is freedom.

Equanimity is taught as the final meditation among the brahma-viharas because it provides the balance for lovingkindness, compassion, and sympathetic joy. These others open one's heart in a wish for well-being: "May you be happy." "May you be free from suffering." "May your joy never cease." Equanimity balances those heartfelt wishes with the recognition that things are the way they are. However much we may wish for something, most results are beyond our control.

When we practice the other three brahma-viharas, we can slip into a sense of owning people and thus trying to manage them. We wish to help, to serve, to heal, to rejoice at the good fortune of others. We might be working to generate a feeling of lovingkindness toward someone, and start to feel impatient with them: "Why aren't you happy yet? Here I am, pouring my heart out for you. Get happy! Start behaving properly."

Equanimity is likened to the way parents feel when their children become adults. The parents have nurtured, have given so much care, have been loving, and then at some point they have to let go. They don't do so with a cold feeling of withdrawal. They don't throw the adult child out of the house, saying, "Well, it was nice, but we don't really need each other anymore." Equanimity has all of the warmth and love of the previous three states, but it also has balance, wisdom, and the understanding that things are as they are, and that we cannot ultimately control someone else's happiness and unhappiness.

This understanding constitutes the words we recite in the equanimity meditation:

> All beings are the owners of their karma.
> Their happiness and unhappiness depend on their actions,
>   not on my wishes for them.

This does not mean that we do not care. We do and we should care. We choose to open our hearts and to offer as much love, compassion, and rejoicing as we possibly can, and we also let go of results. The example might be given of a friend who is engaged in extremely self-destructive behavior. We wish wholeheartedly, with great intensity, that they be free of suffering, that they be happy. But, in the end, we have to recognize where the boundaries actually are, what our responsibility really is, and where the source of happiness truly lies. If that friend does not change their behavior, they will suffer no matter how long and ardently we wish otherwise. Still, we continue to offer them metta and compassion, but we do this with the wisdom and acceptance that they are ultimately responsible for their own actions. In contemporary psychological terms we would call this the release from codependency.

Equanimity's understanding of relatedness helps us to comprehend the profound law of karma. The Buddha called this law "the light of the world," because it illuminates the causes of happiness and suffering and clarifies the path to changing our condition. The Buddha said that karma is so profound that it is actually unfathomable to anyone who does not have a buddha's mental capacities. Chapter 11 of this book, dealing with morality and ethical conduct, will explore this very deep, complex principle more extensively.

For now, one of the simplest possible conceptualizations of karma may be useful for our investigation of equanimity. Imagine the nature of a seed and the fruit that eventually grows from it. If we plant a certain kind of seed, it will inevitably bear the same kind of fruit. An apple seed leads to apples. This is the law of nature. We may plant an apple seed and then beg, weep, and protest because we want to harvest mangoes, but no amount of wishing or anguish will help to get us what we want. If we want mangoes, the only way to get mangoes is to plant a mango seed.

In precisely the same way, the intentions or motives that underlie all of our words and actions plant seeds. Certain kinds of intentions will inevitably bear fruits of the same type. This also is an infallible law of nature. Wholesome intentions—like lovingkindness, compassion, honesty, and respect for the lives and property of others—if they manifest in action will sooner or later bear us the fruits of happiness. Unwholesome intentions—like hatred, cruelty, duplicity—will bear us the fruits of suffering if we express them in words or deeds. No action is without consequences.

When we perform an action, it does not just disappear or evaporate. What we do today will have consequences that we will inevitably experience, either immediately or later. This idea may not seem so abstract or esoteric if we think about the obvious ways that our states of mind bring us feedback from the external world. If you are having a bad day, feeling angry, resentful, fearful, and separate from others, those qualities of consciousness affect how you hold your body, your facial expressions, your speech, and your actions. How do people respond to you on such a day? By contrast, if you wake up filled with gratitude, love, and joy one morning and that mood lasts through the day, how does it affect your appearance, words, and actions? What kind of responses does the world send back?

Sometimes our inner states are reflected by outward circumstances in subtler and more mysterious ways. Many years ago I managed to get myself locked in rooms three times in one week: I went to a friend's wedding and got locked in a storeroom; I attended a workshop and got locked in the bathroom; I went shopping and ended up locked in the shopping mall. All three times the people in charge at these places said, "This has never happened before." I kept thinking, "Well, it has to me!" Something inside my consciousness was manifesting externally. Have you ever had that kind of experience? It is really not so abstract.

As we sow, so do we reap. In this way, karma is the womb out of which we all spring, and everything that befalls us is in some way really ourselves. Thus the intentions that impel our choices of words and actions determine our happiness or unhappiness, not our desires for happiness nor anyone else's desires on our behalf. Karma thus points to personal responsibility, as well as to interrelatedness, and reinforces equanimity in both ways.

Equanimity draws to it and strengthens other liberating mind states. Buoyancy, an agility and pliancy of mind, gives us the ability to relate to each situation as if it were new, with lightness and sensitive resilience, instead of rigidly applying old standards and responses to it. Equanimity also strengthens decisiveness, straightness, honesty, and sincerity of mind, a lack of vacillation and unsettledness. It empowers faith or confidence, the capacity to trust in our actions and our being. Heartened by its inspiration, we resolutely cross the flood without hesitation or looking back. The mind remains tranquil and serene.

As a force that allows us to see things as they are, equanimity gives us the power to distinguish among mind states that may look quite alike but are not really the same. For example, equanimity itself is a state of dispassion that may be mistaken for indifference, equanimity's near enemy in the language of Buddhist psychology. Indifference, a subtle form of aversion, is close enough to look like dispassion at a casual glance. It is not really the same, though, because indifference rests on quiet, sullen withdrawal, which is a type of aversion, and there is no aversion in dispassion's calm sureness.

I often think of dispassion as being a state of great honor, because with it we do not move into a situation with any kind of hidden agenda; there is no manipulation or covert action. There is, rather, a sense of sufficiency. When we can accept a moment or experience as it actually is, out of the resulting sense of stillness, poise, and sufficiency, love can actually emerge.

Equanimity distinguishes guilt from remorse, compassion from aversion. Equanimity endows lovingkindness, compassion, and sympathetic joy with their sense of patience, that ability to be constant and to endure, even if the love, sympathy, or rejoicing is unreturned, even through all the ups and downs. The other brahma-viharas owe their boundless nature to equanimity, that ability to embrace beings impartially.

Thanks to the gift of equanimity, we can develop the courage to stay open to suffering. We can face pain again and again without being overcome by sorrow and misery, without becoming so embittered by them that we have to strike out at them and push them away. In the documentary film *You Got to Move*, about the Highlander Folk School for social change, a woman named Bernice Johnson Reagon reflects on the early sit-ins at lunch counters that sparked so much of the civil rights movement. As college students in the early sixties, she and her friends challenged the racial segregation of public facilities in Albany, Georgia.

> Now I sit back and look at some of the things we did, and I say, "What in the world came over us?" But death had nothing to do with what we were doing. If somebody shot us, we would be dead. And when people died, we cried and went to funerals. And we went and did the next thing the next day, because it was really beyond life and death. It was really like sometimes you know what you're supposed to be doing. And when you know what you're supposed to be doing, it's somebody else's job to kill you.

That is an eloquent example of compassion suffused with equanimity's true courage and the patience to endure. It changes the world.

To have the radiant calm and unswayed balance of mind that we call equanimity is to be like the earth. All kinds of things are cast upon the earth: beautiful and ugly things, frightful and lovable things, common and extraordinary things. The earth receives it all and quietly sustains its own integrity.

It is a state of peace to be able to accept things as they are. This is to be at home in our own lives. We see that this universe is much too big to hold on to, but it is the perfect size for letting go. Our hearts and minds can become that big, and we can actually let go. This is the gift of equanimity.

EXERCISE
Equanimity

The first person we begin to generate equanimity toward is the person said to be the easiest—that is, the neutral person. Holding a sense of this person in your mind, you can recite the equanimity phrases. Traditionally, these are: "All beings are the owners of their karma. Their happiness and unhappiness depend upon their actions, not upon my wishes for them." If you are not comfortable using these phrases, change them however you wish. Some possibilities are:

"May we all accept things as they are."
"May we be undisturbed by the comings and goings of events."
"I will care for you but cannot keep you from suffering."
"I wish you happiness but cannot make your choices for you."

After offering equanimity to the neutral person, the sequence is: the benefactor, friend, enemy, oneself, all beings, . . . groupings, . . . and all beings in the ten directions. Gently recite the equanimity phrase you have chosen, and direct it to each of these categories in turn.

If you feel your mind slipping into indifference, reflect on the fact that equanimity can bring one courage to face change and adversity. Look for subtle forms of aversion and withdrawal. Get a sharper focus on the person or group you are directing equanimity to. Reflect on the immensity of change, and how much things are outside of our control. Then go back to repeating the equanimity phrases.

Once you feel established in the equanimity practice, you can begin to combine it with other brahma-viharas. You can start the sitting by extending lovingkindness, compassion, or sympathetic joy. After some time, switch to equanimity practice. You will find that the spirit of love, compassion, and joy is balanced by equanimity, and that equanimity is enriched by each of the other brahma-viharas. The practice of these four together will lead to a deep feeling of well-being that is not dependent on conditions. Barriers between different parts of ourselves, and between ourselves and others, can be melted, and we can awaken to a new way of living.

10

The Power of Generosity

> If you knew, as I do, the power of giving, you would not let a single meal pass without sharing some of it.
>
> —*The Buddha*

A MEDITATION MASTER from Thailand's forest tradition came to visit the United States several years ago. After just a short time here, he said rather bemusedly, "In Asia the classical sequence of the teachings and practice is first generosity, then morality, and then meditation or insight. But here in the United States, the sequence seems to be meditation first, then morality, and after some time, as a kind of appendix, there is some teaching about generosity. What's going on here?"

Generosity is the inception of the path. The Buddha himself always started with new practitioners by teaching them *dana*, the practice of generosity. This method has remained as the classical tradition of Buddhist teaching. It is often true that we Westerners prefer the enticement of transformative meditative states; we understand the need for effort toward that end and are willing to put it forth. However, the actual springboard for those meditative states is the cultivation of generosity and morality. These qualities, which we consider more mundane, allow those other states to unfold most gracefully and easily.

Generosity has such power because it is characterized by the inner quality of letting go or relinquishing. Being able to let go, to give up, to renounce, to give generously—these capacities spring from the same source within us. When we practice generosity, we open to all of these liberating qualities simultaneously. They carry us to a profound knowing of freedom, and they also are the loving expression of that same state of freedom.

The Buddha said that no true spiritual life is possible without a generous heart. Dana is the very first of the ten *paramis*, or qualities of the awakened mind. The path begins here, and the Buddha began his teachings here, because when we practice generosity, we begin to know a very beautiful quality of joy, a sheer, unhindered delight flowing freely. Giving brings happiness at every stage of its expression. We experience joy in forming the intention to be generous; we experience joy in the actual act of giving something; and we experience joy in remembering the fact that we have given.

Once when I was teaching in Australia, in my discourse on dana I talked about a personal resolve I've made. When a strong urge comes up in my mind to give something—even though the next fifty thoughts may be, "Oh, no, I can't do that. I might need it!"—I give it. Even if fear or other considerations come up, my resolve is to honor that first impulse and to give. One of the students came up to me at the end of the retreat and said that, in honor of that resolve, he wanted to give me some money to give away. He told me that when I got back to the States, when I first landed in California, I should give money to the first people I saw who needed it. I thought maybe he was going to give me thirty or forty dollars, but he gave me hundreds of dollars to give away.

I left for the United States, landed in San Francisco, and the next day I went up and down Telegraph Avenue in Berkeley looking for people to give money to. I wasn't giving away just a dollar; I was giving away ten dollars and twenty dollars. It was an amazing day, just walking around looking for people who needed something. It was such an unusual thing to do that it broke down a lot of barriers between people. There were people literally dancing down the street behind me. It was the most amazingly joyous day for me as well. It is a great happiness to be able to give.

The traditional teachings describe many worldly benefits that come from giving. First of all, when people are generous, others love them. This does not mean that we give so that we will become popular. Rather it is a law of the universe that as we give, we receive.

When you know someone who is very generous, even if she or he has not given to you directly, what does it feel like as you call this person to mind? People who are generous awaken in us openness, love, and delight.

The Buddha also said that people who are generous can enter any group without fear. Part of the delight that comes from giving is in the love we also feel for ourselves. A sense of courage, strength, and brightness grows within us as we learn to give, and it protects us in easy situations and difficult ones alike. People are drawn to us, and their sense of trust in us grows very strong.

There are also spiritual benefits in giving. A single act of giving has a value beyond what we can imagine. So much of the spiritual path is expressed and realized in giving: love, compassion, sympathetic joy, equanimity; letting go of grasping, aversion, and delusion. To give is powerful. That is why the Buddha said that if we knew, as he did, the power of giving, we would not let a single meal pass without sharing some of it.

Sharing food is a metaphor for all giving. When we offer someone food, we are not just giving that person something to eat; we are giving far more. We give strength, health, beauty, clarity of mind, and even life, because none of those things would be possible without food. So when we feed another, this is what we are offering: the substance of life itself.

In a single moment of offering food, the Buddha said, a great part of our spiritual path is fulfilled. All four of the brahma-viharas appear in that moment. Metta, lovingkindness, is there, because we feel goodwill toward the person who is receiving; we want that person to be happy. We feel compassion in that moment, because we wish that being to be free from pain or suffering. We experience sympathetic joy, rejoicing in the person's happiness and wanting it to increase. Equanimity manifests in this act of giving, because we are willing to let go of something we have; we are willing to be without it ourselves. All four of those unique qualities are present right in that one single action.

In that one instant of giving we also abandon the three kilesas, the root tormentors of our hearts. We let go of desire, grasping.

We abandon ill will or aversion, a state that creates separateness, distance, withdrawal, a sense of not being at one with another. And we abandon delusion, because when we perform a wholesome or skillful action like giving, we understand that what we do in our lives, the choices we make, the values we hold, all of these things count for something.

One of the most powerful aspects of delusion, or ignorance, is the belief that what we do does not really matter. To abandon such delusion is to understand the natural law of karma. Despite appearances, nothing is happenstance. We have the power to align ourselves with certain values and to create the life we want by making wholesome choices. When we are generous, life is tangibly and qualitatively different.

When the Buddha spoke of reflecting on our own goodness, he frequently talked about delighting in our acts of giving. It is all too easy for us to dwell on the bad things we have done and said. In the earlier exercises in this book, I asked you to think about some act of giving you had done really well, and asked you to appreciate yourself for having done it. Was that hard for you? You may feel embarrassed to have to sit and reflect in that way. It is so much easier to think about that time you almost gave something but decided not to, while the object is still sitting in the attic.

But to take delight in our generosity helps us immeasurably in our spiritual practice. To recall our gestures of generosity is not conceited or egotistical. Rather, we can see that in this world with its endless choices and possibilities, we care enough about ourselves and others to make the skillful choice. We give rather than hold on; we give up rather than hoard; we let go rather than cling. To take delight in such a choice is another way of taking delight in goodness.

In Burma there is no charge for staying in retreat centers to do meditation practice due to the generous support of the local community. All of the food, for example, is donated. In keeping with this custom of giving food to support free practice, I have made it a point to offer a meal for everyone practicing in the monastery whenever I visit there. There is a part of this that I find very difficult, however. The name of the donor of a meal is posted on a big blackboard outside the dining room. Everyone sees it. Each time I have given a meal, I have had to walk past that board announcing my name in order to get to the dining hall. My first thought on seeing it has been, "I wish this day were over. I wish it were tomorrow! My name is going to be there all day long. I feel so embarrassed and self-conscious. I wish no one knew."

The Burmese do not post people's names in this way in order to make them egocentric. They do it because it is beautiful to give, and they like to hold up beautiful acts so that people can take joy in them and feel inspired by them. It can gladden the heart to acknowledge and remember generosity. If we Westerners can get beyond our conditioned shame and self-hatred, we can enjoy this very special kind of happiness.

Generosity's aim is twofold: we give to free others, and we give to free ourselves. Without both aspects, the experience is incomplete. If we give a gift freely, without attachment to a certain result or expectation of what will come back to us, that exchange celebrates freedom both within ourselves as the giver and in the receiver. In that moment we are not relating to each other in terms of roles or differences; there is no hierarchy. In a moment of pure giving, we really become one. We do not think, "Well, this person has a lot more than I do materially, so what difference does it make if I give them something? Or maybe they don't like me, and here I am about to offer them something, and I feel really foolish." In that one moment of pure giving, all of these divisive, separative attitudes fall away.

When we cut through these differentiations, we remember that our most basic drive, for every single one of us, is a longing to be happy. Engaging in an act of generosity acknowledges our oneness in this wish. How giving enhances this oneness became apparent to me once when I was in a long silent meditation retreat at the Insight Meditation Society. Because I was a founder of the center, I knew everyone on the staff and had a lot of friends in the community. So people who were not themselves in retreat kept leaving little treats for me. Over and over again I would go back to my room to find something placed anonymously outside my door. At times the retreat environment in our tradition can be somewhat austere, so receiving little treats can feel very significant, much more so than it might in normal daily life when such things might be readily available.

With all these gifts coming to me, I began to feel bad for others who were also sitting the retreat but who did not know any staff there. They were not receiving extra things like the ones that were being left for me. So I started to give the little gifts away, to spread them around. I had been especially aware of one person who I thought had probably seen the most things left at my door, so I left something outside her door.

As it turned out, at exactly that same point in the retreat, she started to receive "care packages" from home filled with goodies, and she started giving some of them to me. The treats just kept coming and coming, and I had to keep giving them away to other people. An intense wellspring of affluence had suddenly appeared in the midst of our material austerity! In that time of abundant sharing, when our hearts were so open from the practice we were doing, it felt as if we all really were one. It did not matter where the things had come from, or really even what they were. There was simply an interest in being good to one another, in taking care of one another.

If we practice giving over and over, it grows very strong. Externally, it frees others; internally, we free ourselves. The movement of the heart in generosity mirrors the movement of the heart in letting go on the inner journey. Letting go—abandoning, relinquishing—is actually the same mind state as generosity. So the practice of giving deeply influences the feeling tone of our meditation practice, and vice versa. In this way, generosity establishes the ground in which meditation practice can flourish. The stability of this internal happiness and spaciousness gives us the strength to look at absolutely anything that arises in our heart, and the flexibility to then let it go.

Our conditioning does not emphasize generosity or relinquishing. Wanting, getting, and hoarding are dominant emphases in our culture. A friend told me that starting from the point when she was just learning to talk as a child and continuing all through her childhood, her favorite phrases were "I need it! I want it! I have to have it!" She said these over and over again to her poor parents in all kinds of different situations. When she told me, I thought this is exactly the way it is. This is how we are. We grasp, we cling, we mold things into being exactly as we want them, and then we struggle to keep them that way. This is our normal conditioning.

In the Buddhist cosmology, one of the realms of being is that of "hungry ghosts." These are beings with immense bodies but pinhole mouths, so that they are continually driven by unsatisfied desire. When someone once asked the Vietnamese Buddhist teacher Thich Nhat Hanh what life is like in the realm of hungry ghosts, he answered with one word: "America." The culture we live in, the one that has conditioned us, does not prize yielding, giving up, letting go, relinquishing.

In the Buddhist worldview, the entire conditioned reality in which we live is called samsara: the world of birth and death, arising and passing. This is our life. One of the amazing attributes of samsara is that no matter what we have or what is available to us, we know that somewhere out there, there is always more. The potential for dissatisfaction is infinite, because in this world of change, there is no end to arising and passing away, and the possibilities for comparing and wanting are endless.

I once talked on the phone to a friend the day before he was scheduled to fly to India. The person he was going to travel with had made all the travel arrangements without realizing that for just a small amount of money more, they could have flown business class instead of economy class. On such a long flight, economy class can be quite uncomfortable. So this friend and I were discussing whether they should change their tickets, whether there would be a penalty to do so, how much nicer it would be to make the change and arrive in India rested instead of exhausted and unhappy. Right in the middle of this conversation, my friend suddenly said, "I wonder how much it would cost to go first class." I knew that mind state so well! No sooner have you moved out of economy class and started feeling settled into business class than your mind starts thinking about first class. This is how we are. This is samsara. There is always something else to want.

The preeminent aim of dana is to free ourselves from the conditioned internal forces of craving, clinging, and attachment that bind and limit us. If we are always looking for some object, person, or place to create a sense of completion for ourselves, we miss entirely the degree to which we are whole and complete in every moment. But clinging to samsara is like leaning on a mirage. It cannot uphold or sustain us—there is nothing there. We practice generosity to free our hearts from that delusion, so that we can find and enjoy the force of essential happiness.

So the benefits of generosity are very powerful. As we cultivate it, our heart will stop sticking to things. It is as if we have been making a tight fist for a long time, and slowly the fist opens. We experience relief and happiness as that grip loosens. When the mind becomes suffused with the feeling of generosity, it moves out of a sense of rigid confinement and limitation to a space of being boundless. Our world opens up because we can let go. We can relinquish, and we are not afraid. We do not have to hold on.

This sense of spaciousness is not just theoretical. We can actually watch it develop and grow as we deepen our practice of giving. We continually come up against the limits caused by our attachments, and we can watch them erode. We might begin by feeling, "I will give this much and no more," or, "I will give this object if I am appreciated enough for this act of giving." But as we come to these places that bind or confine us, we learn to see through them, realizing that they are transparent. They have no solidity; they do not have to hold us back. And so we go beyond them. We extend our limits continually outward, creating a deeply composed expansiveness and spaciousness of mind.

The difference between a constricted and an expansive mind state is tangible. Let us say that you sprain an ankle one day. Suddenly you confront pain and the problem of being temporarily disabled, maybe on crutches or in a cast. If your mind feels narrow, confined, and brittle, how do you respond? "Oh, no, I have a sprained ankle. Now I can't go on that hike. I hate being limited like this! No one else has a sprained ankle. I'm such a klutz to have missed that step and sprained it. It's never going to heal right. It will never get any better." In a restricted state of mind, it is very hard to allow those physical and mental discomforts to be there without judging them. On the other hand, if an unpleasant experience arises when our heart is expansive, we do not fear that it will diminish us or that we are a lesser being because of it. We do not have to lament so, because we are not afraid of the experience; we are not greeting it with contraction.

In that quality of openness, when a pleasant experience arises for us, neither do we have to lunge at it in desperation, for we do not need it in order to feel good about ourselves. We can say, "This is the most wonderful gathering of people I've ever been in. That's nice." When it is over, we can let that wonderful thing go, without regret, because within ourselves we feel whole and happy. We understand that we have enough.

We can give in so many ways. We give materially, in terms of goods and money. We give time, service, caring. Even to allow someone to be just the way they are is a kind of giving. We have endless opportunities every day to give. Someone rushes ahead of you for a parking space. Can you give it up, let go, and be happy? If you can, you understand generosity. We do not have to fight and compete with one another nor cling onto things. Instead, we can choose to let go and be really generous with one another.

Generosity allies itself with an inner feeling of abundance—the feeling that we have enough to share. This sense is not based on an objective standard. There are wealthy people who have a strong sense of inner poverty. They find it difficult to stop clinging to their possessions, so it is hard for them to give despite their external abundance. There are economically poor people who are very generous even though from the outside they seem to have nothing to give. But they do not think that way. They give what they can. If you have visited a developing country, you have undoubtedly received a great deal from generous people who are far less wealthy than you are. One of the great joys that come from cultivating generosity is the understanding that no matter how much we have by the world's standards, if we know that we have enough, we can always give something. We can share; we can open; we can express our lovingkindness in this way.

How do we develop this sense of inner abundance? Through my years of spiritual practice, I have held a certain question as my guiding principle: "What do I really need, right now, in this moment, in order to be happy?" In Burma, individuals and families often come from quite a distance in order to offer a meal at a practice center. In that culture, which prizes generosity, to make such an offering is considered a great privilege. It is an opportunity to gain karmic merit, to honor the Buddha's teachings, and to express respect for people who are embodying those teachings by practicing them in meditation retreats.

All of these donors, I am sure, offer the very best they can, in many cases probably better than what they themselves normally eat. But various meals are donated by people from very different economic circumstances. So sometimes I have gone into the dining hall to find a lavish, bountiful feast, with all kinds of Burmese delicacies. And sometimes there is only some bitter vegetables floating in oil.

In Burma we practice very strictly the eight precepts, which means that we eat no solid food after noon. Breakfast happens at about five in the morning, and lunch is served at ten. Thus all eating is over by about ten-thirty a.m., and there is nothing to eat until five o'clock the next morning. Under such circumstances, lunch can feel very important! But it is exactly in this situation that the great value of dana has become clear to me.

In the dining hall at the monastery where I practice, there is an image of the Buddha. Customarily we bow three times before it when we enter the hall. Often I have arrived for lunch and, looking up at that image and bowing, I have felt a wealth of gratitude and joy well up in me. Sometimes when I have looked from the Buddha to the table to see what lunch will be, there has been nothing there that I could eat. I have felt the fear, trepidation, and dread that come from anticipating nineteen hours of hunger.

But then I look at the faces of the people who have provided the food for that meal. They usually come to watch meditators eat what they have given. These people are just radiant! Clearly they are so happy to have had this opportunity to feed us, to offer something to people who are exploring the truth and purifying their minds and hearts.

In less than a minute, I have gone from looking at the Buddha with joy and gratitude, looking at the food with fear and loathing, and then looking at the radiant donors. In that moment, when I have seen how genuinely grateful they are for the chance to give, I have asked myself, "What do I really need right now in order to be happy?" Through this transformative question, I have realized that I am being fed in a much more powerful way by their delight and joy than I am by the food. Clearly such joy flowing from a generous heart is more important, more nourishing.

"What do I need right now in order to be happy?" The world will offer you a lot of answers to that question: you definitely need a new this and a different that. But what do you really lack right now? Does anything really need to change? The whole tenor of spiritual practice is turning things around, deconditioning, getting out of that endless, aching craving. If we have the courage to defy our conditioning, we loosen grasping and clinging and discover an entirely different kind of happiness. What we come to realize eventually is that only something as vast and deep as the truth will really make us happy. And that truth is in this very moment, as we see things as they actually are, as we let go of each state as it arises and passes away, seeing it as it actually is, being able to let go continually as all these different states arise, and allowing them to pass away.

The radiant face of giving is one of the truly beautiful expressions of our own goodness. Let us delight in that goodness. The universal wish to be happy is beneficial; it is skillful; it motivates us to skillful action. Let us rejoice in our ability to make appropriate choices, to cultivate the good, to let go of that which harms us and causes us suffering. This appreciation will give us the confidence and joy we need in order to keep practicing, to keep opening, to keep developing qualities and actions that may feel difficult, unconventional, or unfamiliar to us.

None of us does these things perfectly; that is why we call our efforts "practice." We practice generosity toward others, and we practice it toward ourselves, over and over again. The power of giving grows until it becomes like a great flowing waterfall, until it becomes so natural for us that this is who we are.

EXERCISE

Giving

Another way to understand the teachings of the Buddha as the Middle Path is to understand that the teachings avoid certain philosophical extremes. One extreme states that the world of sense experiences, the world of presentation, of seeing and hearing and tasting, is real and solid. This view seduces us into repeatedly trying to find the singular experience that will give us unchanging happiness. What we have matters a lot from this perspective, and we continue to chase objects or people and try to hold on to them. Especially in a culture of relative freedom and plenty, one can easily become an "experience junkie," ardently trying to experience more and more and have more and more. It is useful to spend some time reflecting on this tendency and whatever role it may have played in your life. Think of the ways you have sought perfect happiness through holding on to someone or something, and the repercussions of that.

The opposite extreme view is a type of nihilism, where we feel that nothing at all matters—everything is empty, fleeting, ephemeral—and we are disconnected and disempowered. Life is seen as meaningless, with no appropriate repository for our faith and no appropriate inspiration for our endeavors. We then overlook the truth that our actions have consequences. We forget that we can and must make effort toward our own release from suffering, and effort toward the release of all beings from suffering. If you have held this nihilistic view at some point in your life, consider the effect it had on your experience of connectedness, empathy, and goodwill. Rather than dwell in this dispirited hopelessness, begin to do metta, compassion, or sympathetic joy meditation. Observe whatever changes arise in your mind.

The Middle Way avoids the extremes of these two views of

materialism and nihilism. Difficult to depict in words, the view of the Middle Way is sometimes best evoked in images, as when the Buddha described life as being like an echo, like a rainbow, like a flash of lightning in a summer's sky, like a phantom, like a dream. The whole world of presentation arises—we see, hear, feel, and so on—and it is also true that nothing lasts, nothing is reliable, nothing has inherent, solid existence.

If we fall into the first extreme view, we will be lost in clinging. If we fall into the second extreme view, we will be lost in complacency or despair. If we rest in the Middle Way, then our actions will reflect an understanding of both the consequential nature of our behavior and the dream-like nature of our lives.

Generosity is primary among the actions of the Middle Way. It allows us to develop the qualities both of nonclinging and of non-complacency. Generosity is the mind's gesture recognizing both that there is nothing solid for us to hold on to and that our actions are meaningful. You can enhance the practice of generosity by observing those moments when the thought of giving does arise and you resist it. Feel the nature of the resistance—paint a word picture of it. Do you experience it as contraction, rigidity, fearfulness? Explore it.

Then examine the impulse to give. What is that sense of yielding, letting go, sharing? How would you describe the nature of the generous intention? Do you notice the release from grasping, the recognition that happiness will not come from holding on and clinging?

If carrying through with the impulse to give a particular object will not create a hardship for yourself or others, see if you can gently drop the resistance and actually offer the object. Even if your motive is a bit mixed, try to stay in touch with all aspects of the action and go on to give the gift. Observe your own mind, and especially follow the thread of feelings resulting from those moments of genuinely letting go and being generous.

Remember that the gift itself need not be glorious, but that giving is a way of stating our interconnectedness. If we undertake generosity as a practice, it will continue to grow ever more powerful. I often think of the quintessential instruction given by Neem Karoli

Baba: "Love people and feed them." For people who took this to heart, it proved to be an important spiritual path.

Once I was accompanying a great meditation teacher on a tour of the United States. As a member of his entourage I was extremely fortunate in being able to spend a lot of time with him. Since his students in various places were happy to see him, they often expressed gratitude for my role in helping facilitate his travels, and they shared their homes and food quite generously. Every once in a while, though, we would be in a situation where the students seemed to regard my presence as a detriment to their own private access to the teacher, and they would tell me they couldn't give me dinner after all, they had run out of food, or something like that. In a strange city, at eight at night, I would set out to find some food. The actual effort to find dinner was no problem, but the feeling of separateness and being unwelcome was very painful. I resolved to try my best not to put others in that position, and to try to live with inclusiveness and sensitivity by that instruction, "Love people and feed them."

In our time, with the prevalent conditioning of self-judgment, it seems important to specifically remember ourselves in our extension of generosity. Giving to others solely motivated by a conviction of our own unworthiness will not tap into the true potential that generosity has to offer us as a vehicle for happiness. The equanimity practice is an important balance for the practice of generosity, so that we are opening, offering, and recognizing present limitations all at the same time. We practice generosity in the context of all four of the brahma-viharas, so that generosity becomes a powerful and expanding expression of the Middle Way.

11

Living Our Love

> . . . with an eye made quiet by the power
> Of harmony, and the deep power of joy,
> We see into the life of things.
>
> —*William Wordsworth*

WE ONCE BROUGHT one of our teachers to the United States from India. After he had been here for some time, we asked him for his perspective on our Buddhist practice in America. While he was mostly very positive about what he saw, one critical thing stood out. Our teacher said that those practicing here in the West sometimes reminded him of people in a rowboat. They row and row and row with great earnestness and effort, but they neglect to untie the boat from the dock. He said he noticed people striving diligently for powerful meditative experiences—wonderful transcendence, going beyond space, time, body, and mind—but not seeming to care so much about how they relate to others in a day-to-day way. How much compassion do they express toward the plumber who is late, or the child who makes a mess? How much kindness? How much presence? The path may lead to many powerful and sublime experiences, but the path begins here with our daily interactions with each other.

All living beings, all of us, want to be happy, yet so few have any idea about how to realize this desire. As I mentioned earlier, this fact is said to be the inspiration behind the Buddha's decision to teach the Dharma. When he looked around the world, he saw beings with this desire for happiness doing over and over again in their ignorance the very things that were bringing them suffering.

Once the Buddha did decide to offer the teachings, he began by teaching people to be generous and to be very careful about what they say and do. If we want to enjoy happiness, taking the care to be ethical is a cardinal means for that aspiration. The Buddha taught that if the heart is full of love and compassion, which is the inner state, the outer manifestation is care and connectedness, which is morality; they are both aspects of the same radiance.

Ethical conduct—*sila* in Pali—is, along with generosity, the necessary foundation for liberation. It is the beginning of the path and is also one of the path's great fruits and culminations. The Buddha taught moral conduct as the source of true beauty, more fundamental than any relative, conventional, or transitory sense of beauty.

Moral conduct is the reflection of our deepest love, concern, and care. The Buddha once said that if we truly loved ourselves, we would never harm another, because we are all interconnected. To protect another is to protect oneself. To protect oneself is to protect another. Sila works on all levels of our relationships: our relationship to ourselves, to other people, and to the environment around us.

Everything is interwoven. The things we do, the things we think about—the things we care about—all make a difference in the totality we are part of. If we want to quiet our minds, to bring our lives into spiritual truth, to see into the life of things, we need to live in harmony.

There is no way to disregard our behavior and then sit down in a formal posture on a meditation cushion and experience freedom, because each part of our life is thoroughly intermeshed with every other part. That is why we consider what the Buddha called "right livelihood" an intrinsic aspect of the liberating path. We cannot engage for eight hours a day in work that involves lying, for example, or harming in some other way, and also feel whole within, unfragmented, when we undertake spiritual practice. Thus we need to look to all of life, to our relationship to all beings, in our aspiration to be free.

The Buddha was an example of a fully integrated being. Compassion, honesty, and wisdom were true for him whether he was alone or among others, wandering or staying still. We have the possibility for just such wholeness and integrity in ourselves as well. We attain it through the practice of sila.

Sila, ethical conduct, rests on aspiring to fulfill certain commitments. Traditionally laypeople in our Buddhist tradition undertake the practice of honoring five basic precepts of conduct:

1. to refrain from killing or physical violence;
2. to refrain from stealing, or taking that which is not given;
3. to refrain from sexual misconduct, or using our sexual energy in a way that causes harm;
4. to refrain from lying, from harsh speech, from idle speech, and from slander;
5. to refrain from taking intoxicants that cloud the mind and cause heedlessness.

Many of us consider ourselves good-hearted people. In fact, I am sure that many of us are indeed good-hearted. So when we hear or read a teaching about morality and reflect on these five basic precepts, many of us feel that as a matter of course we might not kill, steal, rape, slander, or hang out in crack houses. However, I have found in my own life that it is possible continually to refine my understanding of and commitment to these precepts. Honoring them is actually a profound and subtle practice. As we practice them, we discover more and more deeply the levels of strength and protection the precepts can give us.

For example, most of us feel very deeply the gravity of killing other humans, because we feel a sense of connection to what it is to be human; we know the value of human life because we value our own lives. But it is not so easy for us to know and feel our oneness with other forms of life.

We tend to hold the view that the value of life increases according to the size of the being. So we encounter something like a fly and find it easy to kill. When we do not recognize some sense of connection to a fly, it is very easy to do. But is life as it appears in a fly so very different from life as it appears in a human? Does our feeling of separateness from other life-forms actually bring us joy and a sense of wholeness?

If we look carefully and deeply, we can see quite clearly the oneness of all living beings. The Buddha taught that all beings want to be happy. Every single creature of every type and form of life wants to experience happiness. As we come to understand deeply this profound commonality, our relationship to killing of any kind quite naturally changes, and our understanding of the first precept becomes more refined.

To refrain from stealing also has greater implications. It not only means to accept only that which has been offered, but also implies being careful with our resources. If we are so lost in grasping that we are ready to steal, then we are viewing other people, other demands, or other responsibilities simply as obstacles to our fulfillment. We would just as soon push them away in order to get what we want. There is an echo of this feeling of competition and separation even when we are only taking a little of someone's toothpaste or shampoo without asking. Look at what is happening in your mind if you find yourself in that situation—you actually feel quite disconnected from others. A yet more refined understanding of this precept melts barriers of division and exclusivity, reminding us that this entire planet is interdependent and that we have to share its resources.

There is a collection of stories in the Pali literature known as Jataka tales, which are Indian folk stories that depict the previous lives of the Buddha as the Bodhisattva, before his enlightenment. One is about a king who one day offered half of his kingdom and the hand of his daughter in marriage to any man who could steal something without anyone at all finding out about it. This announcement was proclaimed throughout the land, and many young men started showing up with various items. Somebody would come up and say, "I have this ruby necklace that I stole, and nobody knows about it." The king would say, "No, forget it." Somebody else would come up and say, "I have this splendid chariot and I stole it and nobody knows about it." The king would again say, "Sorry, forget it." Everybody got quite confused, until one day a young man showed up with nothing. He said, "I don't have anything at all." The king said, "Well, why not?" The man said, "It is not really possible to steal something with absolutely nobody knowing about it, because I myself would always know about it." This was the right answer. The king had been looking for an heir with wisdom.

We always do know, even if at the time we are acting we do not fully register the fact that we have caused harm; we have planted a seed of pain for ourselves or for others. Somehow we have diminished ourselves and our deepest happiness of connection.

We see the same principle in the precept concerning sexual misconduct. One of my favorite sayings of Sayadaw U Pandita is "Lust cracks the brain." All too often, people will sacrifice love, family life, career, or friendship to satisfy sexual craving. Abiding happiness is given up for temporary pleasure, and a great deal of suffering ensues when we are willing to cause pain to satisfy our desires. Stories abound of adultery, abuse, exploitation, and obsession. These stories illustrate how often our sexual energy is used in harmful ways.

A friend once was at a community meeting at which a member was being rather self-righteously denounced for their sexual misconduct. My friend's comment was, "Who in this room has never made a fool of themselves over sex?" In fact, no one raised their hand. Sexuality is a very powerful force. A mature spirituality demands that we, without self-righteousness, commit to not harming ourselves or others through our sexual energy.

We try not to harm others physically, which means not killing, harming through sexuality, or being abusive or exploitative. We also try not to harm others verbally, seeing that our speech has tremendous power. Words do not just leave our mouths and disappear; they have great effects in this world. We particularly attempt not to lie, because of the delusion that gets generated.

I had an experience some years ago that I think perfectly illustrates the delusion that arises from not telling the truth. At the time, I was living in a house with some friends, and another friend of ours who lived nearby decided to go to India to practice meditation. Because she knew that her mother would worry, she did not want her to know that she was going alone. So she lied by telling her mother that her husband was going to India too, when in fact he was not. She also gave her mother the number at our house to call if any emergency should come up.

About twenty-four hours before my friend was due home from India, her mother called us to ask, "Have you heard from my daughter or her husband?" The person who answered the phone did not remember the lie in that moment, so he blurted out, "Oh yes, her husband was just here for dinner." When he realized what he had done, he tried to set things right by telling another lie. He said, "You know, he went to India with her, but he had a business meeting and came back early for it."

Right away our friend's mother knew that something was wrong, that she was not being told the truth. She panicked. "What aren't you telling me? She's sick, she's very sick, she's beyond sick! What's going on?" My housemate said, "No, no, she's fine. She'll be home in another day."

A few minutes after that phone call, another friend called and said, "Do you know who just called me? Our friend's mother." This woman was so ill at ease about what she had been told that she started calling around the community to see if someone would tell her the truth about her daughter. Now we thought that we had better call everybody before she did, so that we could instruct them as to what lie to tell.

At one point someone none of us knew called. It turned out that the mother had enlisted a neighbor, thinking that if we would not tell her the truth, we might tell someone else the truth. Then we had to call everybody again to alert them about another person who might call, and which lies to tell.

Right in the middle of this whole episode, we began receiving anonymous, obscene phone calls. Normally with such calls we would have just stopped answering the phone. But we had to answer, because someone might call about the situation with our friend's mother, and we had to be ready to tell them the right lie!

Finally one of our friends just gave up. She could not bear it anymore. The next time she talked to our friend's mother, she said, "You're right, we haven't been telling you the truth. This is the truth: the husband never went to India. Your daughter went alone. She's fine. She'll be home in a day."

Two interesting things happened at that point. First, the mother had been lied to so much that she did not believe the truth when she heard it. The other thing was that I saw in my own mind that I had told so many lies by then that I did not know what was true anymore. Confusion reigned. "Did he go to India? What's going on?" I began to see, once again, the power of truth and what it means for another or for oneself to deny that power. In the light of seeing the effects of untruthfulness, we can make a commitment to truthfulness.

One of the points of the precepts is to minimize delusion in all its forms. The last precept is about not taking substances that cloud our mind or cause heedlessness. This concept has been the source of a lot of debate for Westerners. What does it mean to "cloud the mind and cause heedlessness"? What about one little drink if I do not get drunk? I can generally understand such questions. We are each exploring what such commitments would mean, trying to find the balance, the Middle Way that is uniquely right for us at each particular moment in our unfolding.

When I began working with Sayadaw U Pandita, someone asked him about the precept regarding intoxicants: "Is there ever a time when it is all right to have a drink?" I think the question was asked with either the expectation or the hope that U Pandita's answer would be, "Well, it's fine in moderation," or, "You can do it in a social occasion when it would hurt someone's feelings if you did not accept a drink, or when you're visiting your grandmother and she offers you a glass of wine." The actual answer was, "If someone ties you down and pours it down your throat, and you don't enjoy it, then it's all right to have a drink."

I heard that answer and thought, "That's a little extreme!" However, on the strength of U Pandita's words, I later thought, "Who am I just to dismiss what he said? Why not consider it with some humility and take it to heart?" So I decided that, as an experiment, for a period of time I was not going to take a drink. For several years after that decision, I did not drink any alcohol.

It is quite interesting to me that I clearly felt something different as a result of this experiment, which became a part of my practice. I felt as if I had laid something to rest. There was some new clarity and strength, however subtle. I did not feel self-righteous about it and did not go around telling people, "Put down that glass of wine!" or anything like that. It was something inside, a kind of delight I felt within. I felt simpler, stronger, clearer, more confident; I felt more self-respect.

It is very simple but significant in working with these precepts to take the risk of trying such experiments. We find that we can continually refine our understanding of them and can enjoy a deepening sense of radiance and happiness through our attention to them.

To connect to the sources of the happiness that come from being an ethical being, it is crucially important to understand as well as we can the law of karma. In fact, the Buddha said that karma is something we could never fully understand theoretically or cognitively; he called it one of the "four unthinkables." Nonetheless, we can still have an intuitive opening by which we sense at least in part this law of nature.

The law of karma is not the only conditioning force that creates events in our lives, but it is one of the strongest. If we have no sense of karma, it is easy for us to feel victimized by life: "Why me?" We may have a sense of being cursed or blessed, but in either case we feel visited by the circumstances of our lives rather than being a part of them. Comprehending karma is really taking spiritual and moral responsibility for ourselves.

"All beings are the owners of their karma." This is our only true property, the only thing we carry with us from life to life. The vibrational tone of any intention, the motivation behind our speech and action, reflects the kind of seed we are planting in any moment. That intention is the seed, and, given other conditions, the seed sooner or later will bring a certain result. Intentions to help and not to harm bring us results of happiness. Intentions to harm bring us results of some kind of discomfort or suffering.

It is important to understand that the law of karma does not operate with mechanical rigidity. It is not a deterministic process; rather, it actually allows for a lot of variables in the ripening of the fruit. It is as if that seed is planted in a field. The result, the fruit, depends not only on the potential of that one seed, but also upon all of the variable factors of the field. All of our intentions interconnect; they modify and influence one another. Thus, for example, we may tell a harmful lie. The karmic fruit of that action might be greatly intensified if we generally live a life of habitual lying, or it may be quite ameliorated if we generally live a life of truthfulness and compassion.

The Buddha said that because of this complex interaction of mutually modifying conditions, it is incorrect to say that someone will experience the karmic result of an action in just the way he or she performed it. Popular notions of karma might say that if you kill a mosquito, sometime in this lifetime or another you will be attacked by a swarm of mosquitoes. If karma were that deterministic, the Buddha said, then spiritual awakening would be impossible. Basically there would be no opportunity in that worldview to see the end of suffering. But if we say that a person performs a karmic action with a result that can be variably experienced—that she or he will reap the result according to different, interacting conditions—in that case there is the possibility of awakening and the opportunity for making a complete end of suffering.

We continually create a field of influences. We might say that an individual's accumulation of skillful and unskillful karma and also his or her dominant character traits affect karmic results. The very same karmic action may have different results depending on the nature of the field we create to surround it. If we do something unskillful and then we lie about it, that is affecting the field. If, on the other hand, we dedicate our life to restraint, mindfulness, and lovingkindness, the flow of our lives becomes like a vast and open space. Then, even when we do become forgetful or mindless and perform some unskillful action, this karmic cause is being placed in a very different and far more spacious environment.

Thus the Dharma, spiritual practice, protects us. That protection, the creation of a vast openness in which our actions and their fruits occur, comes in part from our cultivation of the brahma-viharas. We develop, as the Buddha advised us to do, a power of love, compassion, joy, and equanimity so strong that our mind becomes like space that cannot be painted, or like the pure river that cannot be burned. Then, even though we cannot escape some karmic effects by hiding in the woods or pulling the blankets over our heads, nonetheless we can ameliorate them by living our lives consciously and with love.

To understand karma does not mean that we become passive about our suffering, that we no longer make an appointment with the dentist when a tooth hurts. We do not say, "Well, it's just my karma," and sit there while the pain deepens. To understand karma means, rather, that we become connected. We have a sense of the reasonableness of our lives. With this feeling of comprehension, we hold our experience differently somehow, with less resentment, bitterness, or clinging. This awareness itself has a tremendous power to lessen our suffering.

In 1991 I attended a conference in India on emotions and health. One afternoon during the conference, the Western psychologists who had had a lot of experience treating victims of torture shared what they had learned about posttraumatic stress disorders. It seemed particularly important to them to pass along their expertise to the Tibetans who were there, because many Tibetans, particularly monks and nuns, have been tortured by the Chinese.

These Western specialists first described what happens psychologically to survivors of torture: flashbacks, hideous memories, terror, helplessness, rage, despair, the sense of being dehumanized and degraded, the experience of feeling isolated and distrustful of others. They went on to discuss how to treat those suffering from these disorders: helping them to work through their fear and rage, and then helping them to feel more reconnected to the community and their own lives. These experts presented their knowledge and reflections with the belief that they were conferring something on the Tibetans: "We want to give you this gift, because we know that the Tibetan people have had to suffer so much."

At the end of their extensive presentation, the leader of the Tibetan people, the Dalai Lama, who was attending the conference, replied, "Well, the Tibetan people do not seem to experience things in quite that way." He explained that though many Tibetans had undergone great physical pain when they were tortured, some reported afterward that they had focused on compassion for the people who were harming them so outrageously. They understood the terrible condition of a mind that would torture another.

He pointed out that even those Tibetans who could not come to a place of feeling compassion while they were being tortured still had a deep belief in and understanding of karma. Thus they had a context in which to view what was happening to them. For them the torture was not a horrid visitation out of the blue. Nor was their understanding based on guilt: "I deserve this." Rather, the victims believed that there was an order, a meaning, a coherence to an experience even that terrible. That is why, the Dalai Lama explained, in his experience Tibetans do not tend to have posttraumatic stress disorder.

Just as karma does not mean blaming ourselves, it also does not mean blaming the victim: "It's just your karma that you're in the gutter. It's really too bad, but you shouldn't have done some awful thing, whatever it was." There is no judgment or sense of withdrawal involved when we grasp karma correctly. True discernment does not separate us from ourselves or from others; it connects us.

Very early in my meditation practice, I experienced some gruesome physical pain, mostly in my knees. When I was sitting in Bodh Gaya, it seemed as if everyone else could sit in sublime peace while I was in agony most of the time. During sittings I would move because of the pain, then move again and again, while others just sat there, still and calm. I felt terrible about not only suffering from so much pain, but also about being the "bad yogi" who moved all the time. At one point I went to my teacher and said in a tone of great self-pity, "Why me? It hurts so much! No one else seems to be suffering."

Munindra blithely answered, "Well, probably in a previous life you tortured many small animals." I thought, "Oh no! That's horrible!" I was only eighteen years old at the time and, while I had not had much of a chance to do a great deal of harm in my life, I nevertheless carried a lot of guilt anyway. Munindra's statement had unintentionally added hugely to that guilt. Whatever I had done in this lifetime seemed bad enough, but the image of me pulling the wings off butterflies and cutting open little creatures in a previous one made me feel much worse. So I added self-lacerating guilt to the physical pain.

I later realized, to my amazement, that my teacher was not judging me at all when he relayed to me this classical karmic explanation for physical pain. His mind did not have even a nuance of separation from me or disgust toward me when he said what he did. To him our lives are merely reasonable; things happen due to causes.

The Buddha himself was asked why people experience such diverse conditions in this world. He replied that we are all the owners of our differing karma and its fruits. Even after death, our only true property is this force of our intentions and their results.

The Buddha said that people who take the lives of others tend to live a short time, and those who refrain from killing tend to live long. People who cause pain to others tend to experience pain, disease, and weakness; those who practice nonviolence tend to experience good health and strength. Those who are greedy and do not give much tend to experience poverty, while those who are generous have abundance. People who are interested and investigate the truth tend to be intelligent; people who do not care about looking more deeply and seeing more clearly tend to be more stupid. Those who practice stealing or adultery do not have many good friends; people who are careful and virtuous in their actions are respected and loved, and they have many friends.

Again, these are not rigid absolutes. They are just tendencies. And there is no judgment in any of it. In the incredible vastness of the vision of buddha-mind, this world of birth, death, and change we call samsara had no beginning. In this inconceivably immense vision of reality, we have all wandered forever, and so we all trail an endless, infinite amount of past karma. Through this timelessness we have all done everything, every one of us: we have loved, hated, feared, killed, raped, stolen, given, served, loved. We have done it all. Through beginningless and ongoing rounds of rebirth, we are all one another's parents, children, friends, lovers, and enemies, over and over again.

There is no reason for a feeling of separation from anything or anyone, because we have been it all and done it all. How then can we feel self-righteous or removed from anyone or any action? There is no spot on this earth where we have not laughed, cried, been born, and died. So in some sense, every single place we go is home. Everyone we meet we know. Everything that is done we are capable of.

That is why we do not hold an understanding of karma in a narrow way. It is an extremely vast vision of life. If at a given moment we experience the fruits of a past action, whether wholesome or unwholesome, our experience is the experience of all beings. If we see an experience happening outside ourselves, we understand that this also is our experience, as in a dream when every character is some reflection of our own mind.

If you do not feel any resonance with this teaching about many lifetimes, you can still understand this radical nonseparation from all who are and all that happens by looking within. Whether or not you believe in rebirth, you can see that all states exist within you. You do not need to feel separate when they arise within you; you do not need to be afraid. And you do not need to feel separate when you see them outside of yourself, either; all of it is just reflecting the mind with all of its possibilities. No matter what happens, inside or outside, no matter whom you meet, all of it is just another way of seeing yourself.

Many years ago I was a nursing student, and in one of the hospital training periods an abused child was brought in, with her abusive mother. There were about thirty nursing students present, plus hospital staff. The students and staff predominantly related to the mother with coldness and aloofness, as though to say, "Oh you beast way, way over there in the distance, how could you have done a thing like that?" Later that day, as the nursing students were gathered, someone made a comment to that effect. I responded by saying, "Well, I could understand doing something like that. I've seen impulses of rage and fear and frustration arise in my mind that could motivate such an awful act. I'm confident I would not do it, because of gifts, such as awareness, that I can bring to bear on that moment, but I don't feel so absolutely, unutterably separate from that mother." Once I had said that, thirty pairs of eyes turned to me and there was complete silence. I sat there wondering, "Did I just say the wrong thing?" But it was clear that although it may have upset the group, it was nonetheless the truth.

Having some intuitive sense of karma—an understanding that our happiness and unhappiness depend on our actions, and that therefore we are ultimately responsible for our fate—shifts our life into a place of empowerment. If we understand that all things, all things whatsoever, arise due to a cause, then we understand safety. Thus, when we see suffering, conflict, danger, pain, or a problem arise in our life, we do not merely try to eliminate it. Rather, we courageously change the conditions that provide the ground for its arising and that support or maintain its existence.

If we look honestly at our lives, we see that the roots of the painful conditions we experience are ignorance, clinging, and hatred. These are the ultimate sources of suffering. With this comprehension, the path we follow is very gentle and very wise, because we see that the suffering, problem, or conflict has no solidity. There is no "solid thing" that holds us in bondage; there is no ultimate reality to the suffering. Actually the suffering is only a combination of conditions. If we change the conditions, we change the problem; if we alter the cause, we alter the effect.

When we work in this gentle but effective way, there is no violence, condemnation, or fear about our situation. There is no confusion about what to do. We stop feeling helpless and powerless. With the utmost gentleness and strength, we can move life in a certain direction, no longer floating along as the victims of circumstance. We change the balance within, and thus change our lives.

A commitment to sila, to morality, protects us because it eliminates the conditions for outrageous defilements to express themselves in our speech and actions. People in this world do behave outrageously toward one another. Whenever I come out of a long meditation retreat, I am terribly shocked just to read a newspaper. It often seems monstrous, what we do to one another. When the forces of grasping, clinging, anger, or delusion get strong enough in anyone's mind, this is what happens.

We all know what it feels like when we have done something we regret and feel we have to keep hidden because it will not bear examination. For example, have you ever spoken about someone in an uncomplimentary way just as that person has walked into the room? Do you remember what that "uh-oh" feeling was like? "Did they hear me? What are they thinking? What will they say about me?" Such thoughts and feelings, as subtle as they can be, harm us in some way. To be free from them frees us from our sense of alienation and separation from others.

Just as we all know what it feels like when we have done something we regret, we all know, too, how it feels when we can stand by our actions with calm self-esteem. That is precisely how a commitment to nonharming is a path to extraordinary happiness. With it we can walk through our lives with dignity, integrity, wholeness, simplicity, lightness, clarity, gladness, peace, buoyancy. We can be at rest, without worry about what other people think of us. There are many stories about people who have gotten enlightened by contemplating their own purity of action, because of the intensity of the joy that comes when we feel confident in this way.

Committing ourselves to caring for one another and living in a way that is not harmful is the most basic and fundamental protection we can give to and receive from each other. It protects us, because if we are not swept up and carried away into actions based on forces such as greed, hatred, and delusion, then we do not have to suffer guilt, remorse, confusion, and trouble in our hearts—now, or even when we die. It also protects others from the harm we might cause them.

The Buddha talked about this effort in the sphere of morality as being a gift of fearlessness to ourselves and to all beings. We give ourselves freedom from fear about the consequences of our actions, either now or later. Instead we feel a beautiful sense of pride or self-esteem that is not convoluted. We give fearlessness to others by becoming trustworthy. Seeing clearly who we are, we serve all beings. As William Butler Yeats wrote, "We can make our minds so like still water that beings gather about us, that they may see their own images, and so live for a moment with a clearer, perhaps even with a fiercer, life because of our quiet."

Having this determination to express our love and compassion through our words and actions does not mean that nothing bad will ever happen in our lives, because very bad things do happen at different times in almost everyone's life. But it does mean that there can be a magic in our lives, in the quality of trust and fearlessness with which we can meet different situations, however bad or difficult.

There is a great difference we can feel between the hesitation and paranoia of not knowing what is correct action and the level of confidence and trust we have when we act from the core of integrity and morality. The ancient texts describe the former situation as "finding ourselves upside down in a pit with no support." Not much fun. The personal power of being confident and clear about our actions and saying what we know without holding back is described in the texts as "the lion's roar."

If we protect the Dharma, the truth of the way things are, the Dharma will protect us. If we support and uphold it, we will be supported and upheld. As we embrace the truth, we are embraced by it, and that is our protection. We find our place of refuge by creating the conditions for it ourselves. This is the law of karma, and our avenue to happiness in it is sila. The Dharma, the way of freedom, is like a hologram: in any single part, we discover the whole. In the brahma-viharas of lovingkindness, compassion, sympathetic joy, and equanimity, we find nonharming conduct; in nonharming conduct, we find the brahma-viharas, the heavenly abodes, that are the revolutionary source of true happiness.

EXERCISE

The Practice of Morality

There are two ways to approach the practice of morality: through developing greater awareness of our motivations and through commitment to the five precepts.

Since all karma is said to rest upon motivation, it is very important that we become increasingly aware of the intentions that drive our actions. Remember that our own motivation can only be truly known by ourselves. Our skillfulness of action might be somewhat assessable through seeing others' reactions to us (though their reactions may be indicative of their own conditioning, far removed from our level of skillfulness). Our motivations, however, can only be reflected to us by the force of our own awareness, directed inward.

As an exercise, we pay careful attention to the intention or motivation that precedes an action. You may experience the intention as a clear directive formed by words in the mind—"Now it's time to have a drink!"—or as an inchoate urge that arises before action is taken. In either case, sit with the intention for a while before deciding whether or not to follow it through. Learn the feeling tone of the vast range of motivations that arise in the mind: love, greed, anger, compassion. Motivations reflect all that we can fear and can want and can love, so the various ways of experiencing them are manifold. The power of our awareness is such that we can open to all of these.

See what motivating force is strongest prior to an action, and explore it without judgment. Does it seem to have a nature that will incline the mind toward suffering, or toward the end of suffering? Toward contraction, attachment, or anger, or toward love, compassion, sympathetic joy, or equanimity? Notice that the decision to follow or not follow an intention into action is a separate and distinct moment from perceiving the nature of the intention itself. Notice that the more fully aware you are of the nature of the motivation, the more you truly have a choice as to whether to act upon it or not.

Making a commitment to following the five precepts allows us to fully acknowledge the range of motivations we see arising in ourselves, without fear that we will act on the negative ones mindlessly. Knowing we can direct our lives either toward complexity and suffering or toward lovingkindness and peace allows us to choose consciously, based on our own understanding.

We make a commitment to each of the five precepts, as we understand them to be, and we commit to continually pay attention—

to our motivations, to our reactions, and to our evolving understanding of a life of lovingkindness. If we lose the power of attention, we lose the intensity and richness of true connectedness in that moment.

A controversial experiment was once done in which subjects were asked to participate in research on the effects of punishment and learning. Each time the person taking the role of learner didn't know the answer to a question, the person taking the role of teacher was to administer an electric shock.

No shocks were actually administered, but the participants did not know that. An actor imitated moans and groans and convincing noises of distress so that the people in the role of teacher would feel they really were administering the shock. They were asked to intensify the shock at every error. The astonishing finding was that 65 percent of the nice, normal people participating in this experiment obeyed the instructions of a "scientist" to keep increasing the shocks despite the "learner's" protests and were willing to deliver enough current to kill the learner.

One possible interpretation of this complex finding is that the incremental nature of the action might have been significant. If the "teachers" had been asked from the beginning to administer enough electric shock to kill somebody, perhaps none of them would have done it. What seems to happen when we take a small step followed by another, and another, is that we lose sight of the whole picture. After that first step, we often don't pay much attention until we've gone a long way down the road. We might then look back and exclaim, "This isn't the road I meant to come down!"

We don't travel far down these roads because we're inherently bad people; 65 percent of us are probably not ready to kill at a moment's notice. We find ourselves unwittingly down these roads because we don't believe we can craft our lives. We find ourselves there because we don't pay attention.

As you grow in the four brahma-viharas, bring them to bear in your life through the five precepts. The precepts provide a language, a vehicle of embodiment for lovingkindness, compassion, sympathetic joy, and equanimity. Make a commitment to lovingkindness and pay attention—you will see a natural ease in following the precepts. Make a commitment to following the precepts, and pay attention—you will see a natural development of self-respect and connectedness to others, nourishing the power of metta and happiness in your life.

Afterword to the 25th Anniversary Edition

When *Lovingkindness* was first published in 1995, it was a different era in the Western appreciation of meditation. Many were skeptical about the usefulness of mindfulness and, I found, even more people were doubtful about the idea of cultivating lovingkindness. That simple wish the Buddha stated in the poem that opens this book—to be "skilled at goodness"—was suspect to some.

At times people criticized the practice of lovingkindness as lacking wisdom. They dismissed those trying to be more kind and loving as weak and sappy, implying that they walked through the world with simpering smiles on their faces, as if lovingkindness made you oblivious to pain or conflict. The question of whether lovingkindness was a weakness or a strength was the first of the major controversies I encountered.

Anyone who attempts to bring kindness more consciously to life sees how much focus and energy is required to begin and to sustain this experiment. The criticism implied that lovingkindness practitioners were falling into a dopey state of bliss instead. Those who have worked on these lovingkindness meditations and exercises have experienced the challenges this practice brings, the big life questions it confronts.

To feel lovingkindness for the world we start close at hand by practicing kindness for ourselves, which is rarely easy and is especially tough at the beginning. Lovingkindness practice shifts us from hyper-criticism to love and compassion, which produces immediate benefits. As our sense of lovingkindness expands, we are more effective, more open and able to learn. This speeds our progress toward our goals. If we make a mistake, instead of criticizing ourselves with the punitive and hostile thoughts we are used to reinforcing, lovingkindness encourages us to give ourselves a break and, in the process, begin to change our damaging habits.

As we practice, we encounter big questions around our ability to love and our worthiness to receive it. With lovingkindness we understand our capacity for love is innate. We don't need to reach out of our comfort zone to "earn" the giving and receiving of love. What we need to do is practice it so that we can feel at home there, even if lovingkindness hasn't particularly been part of our personal or cultural conditioning.

This was the second of the major controversies I encountered: could qualities like love and compassion actually be trained in us?

Buddhist psychology definitely says yes, because it sees qualities like lovingkindness, compassion, sympathetic joy, and equanimity as emergent properties of how we pay attention. The training in these four qualities teaches us how to pay attention differently, which is exactly what meditation is. This is something we are quite capable of doing.

People often come to the lovingkindness practice because of real-life concerns like being unable to let go of a grudge or finding that they feel unable to offer lovingkindness to themselves. As we practice lovingkindness we experience these barriers, one by one, crumbling. By increasing love and kindness in our lives, we are no longer stuck in the reflexive reactions to the events of the day. The connection to ourselves and to the world becomes stronger and more vibrant, and we feel a palpable sense of radiant freedom. With this freedom at the heart of our actions, we experience a reduction in stress and conflict and a heightened sense of the contribution we can make to the world.

Since 1995, more and more scientists have begun to research the effects of lovingkindness, increasingly making the case for the health and psychological benefits of this practice. Taken as a whole, these studies find that lovingkindness, even in small doses, has a profound impact on psychological and physical health.

Barbara Fredrickson, a psychology professor at the University of North Carolina Chapel Hill, has specialized in the study of positive states, often using lovingkindness meditation as the intervention. Her study shows how many of her research subjects who were experimenting with lovingkindness for seven weeks experienced a renewed purpose and satisfaction with their lives and, strengthened by this, felt more social support from others.[*]

An increase in positive states through the practice of lovingkindness may also help with physical pain. In a 2014 study, researchers taught lovingkindness practice to people who suffered from two to ten migraines a month. After a twenty-minute guided meditation session the migraine sufferers reported a 33 percent decrease in pain and a 43 percent reduction in emotional tension.[†] When scientists taught lovingkindness to people who suffered chronic low-back pain, they found significant improvements in pain and stress reduction, with no improvements in the control group who hadn't received instruction.[‡]

These positive emotions and stronger social connections that arise from lovingkindness practice may also affect the aging process. Studies of telomeres, the tips of our chromosomes that protect our DNA from being damaged during cell division, showed that lovingkindness causes them to remain longer. In the most recent study, which was published in 2019, researchers divided up a group of 143 people, teaching a third of them mindfulness meditation, instructing another third in lovingkindness practice, and leaving the last third as a control group. While the telomeres of all shrunk

---

[*] B. L. Fredrickson. "Open Hearts Build Lives: Positive Emotions, Induced through Loving-Kindness Meditation, Build Consequential Personal Resources," *Journal of Personality and Social Psychology* 95, no. 5 (November 2008): 1045–62, https://doi.org/10.1037/a0013262.

[†] Makenzie E. Tonelli and Amy B. Wachholtz. "Meditation-Based Treatment Yielding Immediate Relief for Meditation- Naïve Migraineurs," *Pain Management Nursing* 15, no. 1 (March 2014): 36–40, https://doi.org/10.1016/j.pmn.2012.04.002.

[‡] James W. Carson et al. "Loving-Kindness Meditation for Chronic Low Back Pain: Results from a Pilot Trial," *Journal of Holistic Nursing* 23, no. 3 (September 2005): 287–304, https://doi.orb/10.1177/0898010105277651.

a bit during the study period, the telomeres of those who practiced lovingkindness did not shrink nearly as much. As the researchers wrote, the positive emotions associated with lovingkindness "may have a protective function in reducing cellular aging and maintaining wellness."[*]

Lovingkindness is a powerful transforming practice, but it needs to be practiced, not admired from afar. Everyone has difficulties with any practice at times because we don't know what to expect, or have overly idealistic expectations, or believe that we don't have the time. Perhaps especially with this practice, people may expect that they will soon be flooded with an overwhelming sense of love, and they may be disappointed when they are not.

Yet I am convinced, based on my own experience and that of thousands of people I have taught, that lovingkindness practice is working even if no delightful emotional waves engulf us. Our worldview may be changing, our sense of inclusion may be growing, our fullness of attention may be strengthening without a recognizable, conventional burst of love. In other words, don't be discouraged. The real test of the practice is in our lives. How are we when meeting a stranger? How do we speak to ourselves when we've made a mistake? If we've categorized someone and dismissed them out of hand, are we willing to take another look? Practice is important, and it is a gift to the world to choose to begin and to continue.

A student once took me out to lunch in New York City and confessed, "I've been practicing lovingkindness as my main practice for about three years now, whether I'm on a retreat or doing my regular morning practice. In some ways, my experience sitting now is not all that different from what it was in the beginning, but I'm like a completely different person. I'm different with myself, and with my family. I'm different ethically, and with my communi-

---

[*] Khoa D. Le Nguyen et al. "Loving-Kindness Meditation Slows Biological Aging in Novices: Evidence from a 12-Week Randomized Controlled Trial," *Psychoneuroendocrinology* 108 (October 2019): 20–27, https://doi.org/10.1016/j.psyneuen.2019.05.020.

ty." Then he looked at me and added, "Is that enough?" I started laughing and said to him, "Yes, I really think that's enough. Still having bouts of sleepiness or restlessness in formal sitting and being a completely different person relating to oneself and others is a pretty good result!"

The practice is in itself a revolutionary disruption of the norm that teaches us to be disconnected, fearful, or resentful, and then somehow we will be safe. In fact, the opposite is true. The practice of lovingkindness is one that brings many benefits to us and to the world. It gives us the ability to take abstract ideals like compassion or "love thy neighbor" and make them real each and every day, going to work or to school, leaving home, or getting through a situation we would never in a million years have chosen. Connection, balance, care, and joy can truly form the basis for our strength and safety, and the foundation for, as the subtitle of the book says, *the revolutionary art of happiness*.

A friend of mine once mused, looking at a rather depressing landscape painting, "This looks like a world that could use some love." Her comment has stayed with me through the years as I look at the world—how badly we can at times treat other people, or animals, or the planet. It has always looked like a world that could use some love, and perhaps most especially now. The need for greater connection seems so acute, and I feel blessed to have been offered tools, and have the chance to offer tools to others, with which we can go deeper than the abstract or merely philosophical and work to bring lovingkindness to life.

For More Information

Readers who desire information about Insight Meditation retreats and teaching worldwide may contact the Insight Meditation Society, 1230 Pleasant Street, Barre, Massachusetts 01005, or at *www.dharma.org*. For information about Insight Meditation audio and video recordings, please visit www.dharmaseed.org.

Credits

I wish to thank the publishers who granted permission to reprint the following excerpts:

From *The Enlightened Heart*, edited by Stephen Mitchell ("Ten thousand flowers . . ." by Wu-men and "In the cherry blossom's shade . . ." by Issa), © 1989 by Stephen Mitchell. Reprinted by permission of HarperCollins Publishers, Inc.

From "Keeping Quiet," from *Extravagaria*, by Pablo Neruda, translated by Alastair Reid. Translation © 1974 by Alastair Reid. Reprinted by permission of Farrar, Straus & Giroux, Inc.

From "Musée des Beaux Arts," from *Collected Poems*, by W. H. Auden, © 1940 and renewed 1968 by W. H. Auden. Reprinted by permission of Random House, Inc., and Curtis Brown Ltd.

From *One Robe, One Bowl: The Zen Poetry of Ryokan*, translated by John Stevens, © 1984 by John Stevens. Reprinted by permission of Weatherhill, Inc.

From *Rumi: These Branching Moments*, by Coleman Barks and John Moyne, © 1988 by Coleman Barks and John Moyne. Reprinted by permission of Copper Beech Press.

From "St. Francis and the Sow," by Galway Kinnell, from *Mortal Acts, Mortal Words*, © 1980 by Galway Kinnell. Reprinted by permission of Houghton Mifflin Co. and Jonathan Cape Ltd. All rights reserved.

About the Author

SHARON SALZBERG is one of America's leading spiritual teachers and authors. She is cofounder of the Insight Meditation Society in Barre, Massachusetts. She has played a major part in bringing Eastern meditation practices to the West. She was a contributing editor of Oprah's *O* magazine, and her writing has been featured in *Time, Yoga Journal, Real Simple, Body & Soul, Self, Buddhadharma, More,* and *Shambhala Sun*. Various anthologies on spirituality have featured Sharon Salzberg and her work, including *How to Stop the Next War Now: Effective Responses to Violence and Terrorism*. She has addressed audiences at the State of the World Forum and the Peacemakers Conference, and has delivered keynotes at Kripalu and Omega conferences. She teaches meditation around the country, online, and abroad, and has been practicing Buddhist meditation for over forty years.